A Place And A Time

by
James Etheridge

Edited by
Jackie Stokes

A Place And A Time
James Etheridge

If you would like to order books from the author or
do any of the above, you may contact the author via
AquaHue Artworks at aquahueartworks@earthlink.net

Cover artwork and design by James Etheridge.
All rights reserved.

A special thanks to Judy Wills Lowder
for her help in the publication of this book.

For Jackie
For your constant love and support.
Without you, there would be no art.

Stacey
For your encouragement and for the opportunity.

Mr. Almand
For teaching me to read and to write.

And for
Chip

Table of Contents

Ecclesiastes 3:1-8

Preface

I was four years old in December of 1959. Unbeknownst to me at the time, one of the greatest things that ever happened to me took place. My parents and I moved from East Atlanta to Gresham Park. Gresham Park is a community in DeKalb County, about ten miles east of Atlanta. It was developed in the early 1950s. The house that I grew up in was built in 1955, the year that I was born.

My father grew up in East Atlanta. His parents had moved from the Winder area in the early twentieth century to seek better opportunities in the city. My grandparents lived down the street from us in East Atlanta. My aunt, uncle and three cousins lived behind us. Another aunt, uncle and two cousins lived one street over. Daddy worked for the City of Atlanta Fire Department. When he bought the house in Gresham Park, everyone asked him, "Why are you moving way out there?" The monthly house note was $90 and my grandfather told him that he was going to lose every penny he had.

Before the development of Atlanta moved east in the years after World War II, most of DeKalb County was wilderness. There were a lot of woodlands, a lot of pastures and a lot of dairy farms. Gresham Park itself was originally dairy land and was called Parker Ranch.

The Parker Ranch dairy land was located in the area east of what is now Parker Ranch Road, which runs off of Gresham Road. This was the location of a huge meadow from which the name Meadowview Drive was derived.

I made and have maintained lifelong friendships with many of those that I grew up with in Gresham Park. We have had discussions as to just how fortunate we were to have grown up in such a place and a time. We laughed. We cried. We lived. We died. We won. We lost. We experienced joy. We experienced heartbreak. We worked. We played. We had disagreements. We had understandings. We were praised. We were punished. We learned firsthand to live life.

We all went to school together. Sometimes they were different schools, but we all went to school together. The elementary schools were Gresham Park, Meadowview, Clifton, Bouldercrest, Kelly Lake and Sky Haven. The high schools were Walker and Gordon. A few of the neighboring schools were Southwest DeKalb, Columbia, Cedar Grove, East Atlanta and Roosevelt. We hung out at McDonald's and Dairy Queen in our souped up cars. We went to the movies at the Madison Theatre in East Atlanta, The Belvedere in Decatur and The Starlight Drive-In on Moreland Avenue. We rolled yards and put potatoes in exhaust pipes. We strung rubber chickens up our rival school's flagpole on the eve of a big game and mooned their cheerleaders' bus on the way to the stadium. We voted for homecoming queens, class presidents and team captains. The principals, teachers and coaches had paddles and weren't afraid to use them. There was no need for metal detectors or police presence. Occasionally the hoods that were smoking in the boys' room would flush a cherry bomb down the toilet. A lit cigarette tossed in a trash can set one of the bathrooms on fire once and the fire department was called. That was about the extent of juvenile delinquency.

We kids could walk or ride our bikes to and from school, to the store for candy and Cokes, to the park to play and to visit one another's houses. We went trick or treating alone for hours on end on Halloween night. We played ball at the ballpark and in our back yards. We were outside from morning until evening, when our mothers would call or whistle us in for supper. We swam in Sugar Creek and at Clifton Springs. The doors to the houses were never locked. There was no need.

Families would come and go. Some would move in. Some would move out. Some would move two streets over. I could not guess at a population. Whatever the number, everyone pretty much knew everyone. For many others and myself, Gresham Park was the center of the universe. It was a place and a time which we all took for granted those many years ago.

The Very Heart

I grew up at 2796 Rollingwood Lane, in the very heart of Gresham Park. I never realized it until I looked at a map years later, but 2796 is literally at the geographical center of Gresham Park. Rollingwood Lane was a main thoroughfare through town, connecting the north side to the south side. There was a bus stop at the end of our driveway. My mother and I would walk to the end of the driveway and catch the bus. We would ride to Rich's downtown for shopping and lunch at the Magnolia Room. The bus would then bring us home and drop us at the end of our driveway. In the bliss of my youthful naiveté, I thought all anyone had to do to catch the bus was to walk to the end of their driveway.

I grew up as an only child. But there were neighborhood kids all around, so I was never alone and certainly never lacked for companionship of my own age. There were neighborhoods in the community and there were neighborhoods within the neighborhoods.

My best friend in our neighborhood was Billy, who lived directly across the street. Billy and I played ball, built model cars and airplanes, shot our BB guns, rode our bicycles and built coaster wagons. We played in the elementary school band together. I played the saxophone and he played the trumpet. After we started high school, I put down the sax and picked up a football. Billy kept at it and became Second Chair Trumpet in the band. His family moved to South Georgia when we were in the tenth grade. I saw him once after they moved. His family came back up to Atlanta to visit friends. Billy and his older brother came by to visit. I never saw him again, but heard that he had moved to California, became a software engineer for Adobe and had done quite well for himself.

Brain lived next door to Billy. Brain got his name on the first day of school in the fourth grade. His real name, Brian, was misspelled on the roll. The teacher called out "Brain Fowler" and he immediately and forever became "Brain." Even the girls called him that. At a high school reunion years later, they put "Brain" on his name tag because nobody knew him as Brian. Everybody knew him as Brain.

Brain introduced me to Monopoly. He and his little brother, Joey, would bring the Monopoly board over to my house at least once or twice a week during the summer. We would play for hours in our basement den. Brain was a tremendous athlete, even when we were kids. His first love was baseball. At age eight he was already hitting two hundred and fifty foot line drives and could run through a defensive line of guys five years older than him like they were tackling dummies. He became an All-State linebacker in high school, but his first love was baseball. He was drafted by the Cubs and spent ten years in the minors before hanging up the cleats.

Bubba-Bubba lived down the hill to our right. He was technically my next door neighbor, but his house was about a quarter of a mile down the hill on the other side of the woods. Bubba-Bubba was a year older than Billy, Brain and me. He was also the shortest and had a textbook case of the Napoleon complex before anybody knew what that was. He was called Bubba-Bubba because that was what his baby brother called him. He always wanted to be in charge and call the shots. We all eventually outgrew him and quit paying him any mind. His family moved away after he graduated high school. The last I heard of him he was working for the post office.

Jane lived across the street from Bubba-Bubba. She was about five years older than us, the high school cheerleading captain and drove a little blue Sunbeam Alpine. She would blast past us with the top down, her long black hair flying, toot the horn and wave at us. We would sit there on our bicycles with our mouths hanging open, staring blankly and attempting weakly to wave back.

Anna lived across the street from me and two doors down from Billy. She was the first girl I was ever friends with. Anna was a tall girl and very intelligent. She loved animals and could run like the wind.

Two doors up from us lived an older couple, Mr. and Mrs. Jenkins. They had a white English bulldog named Sluggo. Sluggo lived like a king. His doghouse in the back yard had a front porch with a roof. It also had a fan and a heat lamp installed in it, with the wires buried and running to switches in the kitchen. In the summer, Mrs. Jenkins would turn his fan on and cool the doghouse. In the winter when Sluggo got cold, he would bark and she would turn his heat lamp on.

Sluggo was my buddy. I would walk up through my next door neighbor Jake's back yard and visit him at the fence. He was solid white and I did not know then that my friend was special. At that point, the only English Bulldogs I had ever seen were Sluggo and UGA, so I thought all English Bulldogs were white. I was not aware that they are very much the exception. Sluggo was one of the greatest dogs I ever knew and I still love him today. When we moved from Gresham Park, the hardest thing was saying goodbye to Sluggo. I stood at the fence, eighteen years old, hugging him and crying like a baby. I promised him that I would come back and visit. I never did. I only hope that Sluggo is waiting for me on The Rainbow Bridge.

Speaking of dogs, Billy had an American Bulldog named Socko. He was the neighborhood dog. Socko looked mean but was completely gentle, never barked and didn't bite. The only problem was that he had a propensity to chase cars. One day he caught one. Billy's dad buried him in the back yard. It was a National Day Of Mourning in the neighborhood.

We played in the street all the time. It is a miracle no one was hit or run over. Buses flew down the street. Cars traveled up and down it all day. And we were right out there in the middle of it on our bikes, coaster wagons and skateboards.

We played backyard ball year round. Army maneuvers were carried out in the woods as well as squirrel hunting with our BB guns, exploring, camping and catching crawfish and salamanders in the creek. Miraculously, we never saw a snake, at least not to my knowledge.

The ice cream truck came by every Wednesday at noon. I can still hear the music it played over the loudspeaker. We would stand at the end of our driveway and you could see it cross Rollingwood on Boulderview Drive at the top of the hill. After what seemed like an eternity, it would re-appear and turn down our street.

At the bottom of the hill were paths leading into the woods on the other side of the street from our woods. We would ride our bikes on the paths all the way to Sugar Creek. Sugar Creek is a large creek that meanders from East Atlanta through South DeKalb County before emptying into the South River. We would go swimming in Sugar Creek with no thought of snapping turtles, water moccasins or copperheads. In those non-environmentally safe times, Sugar Creek and the South River became somewhat polluted. Big bergs of soapsuds would float by us as we swam. We thought it was funny.

At the very top of the hill lived The Girl. I had my first schoolboy crush on her. I used to walk or ride my bike up to her house and talk to her through her screen door. Boys were not allowed in the house, you see. The Girl was a little lady.

I have not since lived in a neighborhood such as Rollingwood, nor will I ever again. We were all fortunate to grow up in Gresham Park and some of us were even more fortunate to grow up on Rollingwood. As kids, everything that we could need or want was right there outside of our doors. The memories are there. They always will be.

The Ballpark

There were two summer Meccas in Gresham Park. One was Clifton Springs and the other was the Gresham Park Recreation Center, better known as the ballpark. Kids and parents alike flocked there. There were baseball leagues in the summer and football leagues in the fall. The Civic Center building contained a gymnasium, the director's office and a meeting room. In the meeting room was a ping pong table as well as a bumper pool table. That was the first place I ever saw bumper pool. I didn't understand the concept then and not sure that I do now.

The first organized sport I played was baseball. The ages were from eight to eighteen, and the rules regarding such were not as cut and dry as they are now. First, there was the Minor League. The Minor League's team names were taken from the old Southern League. There were the Barons, the Smokies, the Chicks, the Travelers, the Pelicans, the Lookouts, the Sports and the Bears. I played on the Barons and was the youngest player on the team, seven years old when the season started. Most of the other boys were a year to two years older than me. There was one boy on our team who was four years older. It all depended on a kid's ability and where he fit in most comfortably. The next league up from the Minor League was the Major League, whose team names were taken from the American League. The Babe

Ruth League played on the big field up the hill, as well as the Connie Mack traveling team that was made up of seventeen and eighteen year olds. The football field was across Gresham Road from the two main baseball fields. In the spring the northeast corner of the football field was converted to the girl's softball field. The southeast corner was also converted to a second minor league baseball field.

Some of us had never played baseball in our lives and our coaches were very patient. They taught us the basics of the game and let us all play, even if it happened to be right field. We played real baseball right out of the chute. The coaches didn't pitch to us, except in practice. We played six innings and there was no run limit. The second year I played we beat the Smokies 39-5. It was a good lesson learned though, because the next time we played them we thought all we had to do was show up. They beat us 21-3. Touché. There were a lot of walks and a lot of swinging strikeouts. There was no six pitch limit. You either got three strikes, four balls, or a hit. I remember vividly my first hit, a dribbling grounder into no man's land between the pitcher's mound and third. I managed to beat out the throw and a few minutes later, I scored my first run.

The ballpark was always full, thriving and hopping. We would ride our bikes there or our parents would drop us off to spend the day. When a foul ball was popped over the fence, there was a huge scramble to retrieve it. The lucky kid that got the ball would go to the concession stand, get a free Coke and return the ball to the umpire. Pixie Stix, Sour Grapes, Sour Apples and Atomic Fireballs were also available at the concession stand. Sour Grapes and Apples were bubble gum balls about three quarters of an inch in diameter and were both sweet and sour at the same time. Pixie Stix resembled paper drinking straws and contained what amounted to Kool-Aid powder and sugar. Atomic Fireballs were just that, hard red balls the same size as Sour Grapes and hotter than a habanero. We would fill the back pocket of our baseball pants with Sour Grapes, Sour Apples and Fireballs. During the game we would load up our cheeks with one or more of each, thinking we were just like the cool players on the CBS Saturday Game Of The Week.

Moms took turns working in the concession stand. Dads and older brothers would announce the batters and lineup changes over the PA system and work the scoreboard. The second minor league field had a hand operated scoreboard and the numbers were changed manually. Coaches would recruit kids, dads or both from the bleachers to work it. That was where I learned to score a baseball game.

Behind the Major League field were the tennis courts and a covered picnic area. To the right of that was the Pee Wee field. The Pee Wee League was started a couple of years after I started playing baseball. It was a smaller field with forty foot baselines. The players' ages were six and seven and it was real baseball as well. There were no hitting tees and no coaches pitching. Nine players were on the field for each side, and the pitcher got up and took his cuts just like everybody else.

The Powder Puff League was the girl's softball league and it was anything but Powder Puff. It was all fast pitch, no slow pitch. The infield was solid red Georgia clay. The girls all wore shorts with knee high socks.

When I was eleven years old, we were playing a game on the Major League field. I was playing first base. We heard a crashing sound through the treetops on the third base side and a ball landed on the infield between first and second base. The Big Kid had hit it from the Babe Ruth field above us. He was fourteen at the time. From home plate to where the ball landed is a distance of roughly five hundred feet. From what I've been told, it was neither the first nor the last time he cleared the trees behind the left field scoreboard. The Big Kid was the number one overall draft pick out of high school and spent eleven seasons in the Majors.

The football field was a flood plain for Sugar Creek. There was no drainage system so when it rained, you would sometimes be up to your ankles in standing water. While this made for a grand time of playing in the mud, it was no fun for the guys running with the ball. The

DeKalb Yellow Jackets was the traveling team. There was an intramural league consisting of four teams, the Wasps, the Bees, the Hornets and the Gnats. I played on the Wasps. Our colors were green and white and I still have my old uniform. All the teams played under the Georgia High School Association rules. Full speed. Blocking. Tackling. No coaches in the backfields during the game. Real football.

The gymnasium was a basketball court with the lines inlaid into a tile floor. I played many a pickup basketball game there. Though it's no fun to fall anywhere, it really was no fun to fall on that tile floor. Three feet from the out of bounds line was the painted cinderblock wall. Crashing into it going out of bounds could mean a separated shoulder, a broken nose, a chipped tooth or all of the above. The gymnasium was multi-purposed and really served as the defacto town meeting hall. There were civic meetings there as well as political rallies, banquets and parties. Baseball, softball and football team pictures were taken in the gym as well as yearly family pictures. Booths were set up in there during the annual carnival. The Boy Scouts, Cub Scouts and Girl Scouts held their meetings there also.

There was a basketball league at the gym. There were four teams in the league and the games were played on weekday afternoons. My friend Jack played in the league and would catch the bus after school, ride to the gym for a game and then catch the bus back home.

The pickup games we played in the gym as teenagers were somewhat of a cross between basketball, lacrosse and rollerball. Full contact, no refs, no clock, no nothing. Guys from other areas would show up, get in the game and then leave after about ten minutes or so.

High school homecoming parades started at the ballpark. All of the floats and cars would gather there, along with the marching band, drill team and majorettes. The parade would proceed up Clifton Church Road, take a right on Clifton Springs Way, a right on Clifton Springs Road and all the way down to Panthersville Stadium.

In the early Seventies, the Yellow Jackets moved east to Browns Mill Park. A new baseball and football complex was built a mile or so away. The dugouts were eventually torn down at the baseball fields and the fences and backstops removed. The tennis courts were torn up. A big, new state of the art gymnasium was built next to the old one. The football field was turned into a parking lot. The baseball diamonds are just grassy fields now. The times that I've ridden by, I've never seen anyone on either one of them. But as I slow down and I look, I can see us there. I see Herb pitching. I see myself on first base. I see Duke in center field and Scooter at shortstop. I see Banana Nose attempting to call the balls and strikes. I see the coaches in the first and third base boxes. I see The Big Kid at the plate, ready to launch another rocket. I see us all. We're on our Field of Dreams. The memories are there. They always will be.

Clifton Springs

In the Fifties, as the suburbs of Atlanta moved east, several family playgrounds sprang up. There was Misty Waters in Decatur, Glenwood Hills across from East Lake Golf Club and Clifton Springs in Gresham Park. Clifton Springs was built in the Fifties and flourished into the early Seventies. It featured a one acre swimming lake complete with a large white sand beach, a dock in the middle with a diving board and a twenty foot platform that was two levels with a diving board at the top. The diving board at the top was not for the faint of heart. There was a golf course, a driving range, a bowling alley and a miniature golf course. There was also a children's area featuring a small carousel, a Briggs and Stratton powered Ferris wheel and a miniature train that ran through the woods. My father and uncle laid the tracks for the miniature train. In later years the bowling alley became a slot car track.

As far as my seven year old mind knew, Clifton Springs was the beach. There was sand and there was water. There were transistor radios and teenage girls in bikinis. There were kids building sand castles and couples sunbathing. My parents and I would go there Saturday or Sunday afternoons, have lunch at one of the picnic tables in the shade and lounge on a blanket on the sand. I would play in the water with all the other kids. My father would stand guard near the rope that separated the shallow end from the deep end.

I was eight years old the first time I saw the ocean for real. We were on our way to Fort Pierce, Florida to visit my aunt, uncle and cousins. This was before I-75 and the Sunshine Parkway, so we traveled down US 1 and stopped at Daytona. My father parked our turquoise and white '59 Ford on the beach. I climbed out of the back seat in my swim trunks, ran and dove into the water. The shock of the salt hitting my eyes, nose and mouth took my breath away. I came up gagging. I thought I was diving into the water back at Clifton Springs. No one had told me that the ocean was salt water. Imagine how I felt later when I found out that the moon wasn't really made out of green cheese.

As we grew older we would ride our bikes to Clifton Springs or our parents would drop us off. I think it cost fifty cents to swim all day and we didn't have to sign any waivers or releases. The attendant would put your belongings in an individual wire basket behind the counter, then give you a colored cloth tag to pin onto your swimsuit. There was a different color for each day. You would walk past the jukebox room where all the hoods hung out smoking cigarettes. At the gate one of the lifeguards checked your cloth tag. Then you were off to the docks and the diving boards.

Summers in Gresham Park there were two places to be, Clifton Springs or the ballpark. Each was jam packed every day. For many of us, our first exposure to golf was at Clifton Springs. The tee boxes were concrete with black rubber mats. It was also lighted so you could play at night. The first time I ever played golf was there at night. I was with Billy. We were twelve and shared his older brother's clubs. Miraculously, we didn't bend or break any of them.

And there were the cars. The driveway went past the golf clubhouse, down the hill to the lake, across the dam, atop the wall behind the beach, into the parking lot behind the clubhouse and back up the hill. There was always a steady stream of cars around the driveway.

My father and I built a Meyers Manx dune buggy. It had a beefed up VW engine with chrome headers. The transmission was a modified transmission out of a Microbus. The car would only go 70 mph but would get there in a hurry. I found out later that it would yank the front wheels up off of the ground in first and second gear. That would prove to be my undoing.

One Sunday afternoon my buddy Moon and I were at Clifton Springs and I was bragging that the dune buggy could do wheelstands. No one believed me. A scoffer challenged me to prove it. Moon and I climbed into the buggy with a small crowd gathered around. I got it rolling backwards down the hill, revved up the engine and dumped the clutch. The front end jumped off the ground and we tore off up the hill. I hit second gear and the front end popped up again. We took a left out of Clifton and buzzed into the subdivision across the street. As I slowed for a stop sign Moon looked at me and said, "Now look in your rear view mirror." My father was flying up behind me in my mother's yellow Ford Fairlane, hanging out the window and screaming at me to "take that blankity blank thing home right now!" "I've got to take Moon home first," I called back. "Well, take his [gluteus maximus] there and then get yours home!" he yelled. I found out later that the old man made a habit of following me from a distance. How else would he have known that I was doing wheelstands at Clifton Springs and just happen to come riding up behind me? When I got home my mother told me that my father was in the basement waiting for me. I went downstairs and he demanded my driver's license. I gave it to him and he tried to rip it in half. He couldn't and I laughed. That was the wrong thing to do, but he looked funny trying to rip a laminated plastic license in half and turning blue in the process. When I laughed he looked at me with his eyes on fire and his face turning a deep purple. He snatched up a pair of tin snips and cut my license up into confetti. Then he yelled something about there it was on the floor and my blankity blank future along with it. He stormed out, presumably to go smoke a half a pack of Lucky Strikes at once. That was the last time I drove the dune buggy. It was sold within two weeks.

Time marches on and things change. Misty Waters became an apartment complex. Glenwood Hills was developed into a subdivision. The beach at Clifton Springs was shut down. Sometime in the mid Seventies the lake was drained. A big, new swimming pool was built behind the gym in Gresham Park. It was a nice pool, but it wasn't Clifton Springs. It never could be. Clifton Springs was a place and a time that was gone forever.

The golf course survived into the early Nineties. The property was sold and the new owner cleared out the lake, re-filled it and built an island green in the middle. It was about a 135 yard shot from the tees, which were in the middle of where the old beach parking lot had been located. The green was not easy to hit. I played in a couple of leagues there and won my first golf trophy for third place in the B division. It is the one golf trophy with which I could never part. Not because it was my first but because it's from Clifton Springs.

A mega-church bought the property, but you can still see some of the tees and greens. The lake is still on the property, at the back behind the church. It makes me happy to know it is still there. But I wish I could ride in my dune buggy one more time down the hill, across the dam, around the wall and through the parking lot. No wheelstands, though. The memories are there. They always will be.

Grammar School and Girls

The Gresham Park Elementary School Eagles was the name of my grammar school and our mascot. I'm not sure why we had a mascot because we didn't have any sports teams, other than the ones that were picked at recess. Political correctness was unheard of back then. Some kids got picked for teams and some didn't. The ones that didn't were divided up between the two teams. We played dodgeball. We played kickball. We played on the monkey bars. Somehow, we survived.

Gresham Park Elementary was in the middle of a neighborhood, located at 1848 Vicki Lane. How "Vicki Lane" came to be named as such is an interesting story. The street was unnamed in the early development of Gresham Park. One of the original residents was working in his yard one day and one of the developers stopped by and asked him if he would like to name the street. "Sure, Vicki Lane," he replied and the street was named after his daughter.

The school was built and opened in 1958. It had a capacity of about two hundred and fifty students. Our school colors were green and white. I still have a green and white beanie that was sold by the PTA one year. It has "Gresham Park School" on it. I'll put it on from time to time to get a laugh out of the kids and the adults as well. We would get fold up book covers for free at the dime store at the beginning of the school year. Ours were green and white. Meadowview's were red and white, Sky Haven's blue and white. Meadowview was our rival school, I guess, if a grammar school can have a rival school.

My mother taught kindergarten at Davis Kindergarten and Nursery which was located about a mile and a half from the school. One of her duties was driving the Panda Bus. The Panda Bus was a 1960 Volkswagen Transporter Microbus. There were actually two of them. Each had Panda faces painted on the front with black and gray trim and lettering on the side. My father painted both buses. He also built and painted the background scenery of a large shoe with a door for our kindergarten graduation program. The program was "The Old Woman Who Lived In A Shoe." I was Jack and a blonde girl with cat-eye glasses was Jill. My mother was convinced that one day Jill and I would get married. For all of this work my father was given a Sears Craftsman Saber Saw. He was a shrewd businessman. I have the saw and it is still operational. Momma would pick up kids at their houses in the Panda Bus and take us to school. She would then pick us up in the afternoon and take us back to the nursery, where parents would pick their children up on the way home from work.

There were no junior highs in DeKalb County back then. Grammar schools were first through seventh grade, high schools eighth through twelfth. I still remember my first day of school in the first grade. Kids were screaming and blubbering when their parents left. I was a big boy. I didn't cry. I also remember being a little incredulous that kids were actually crying. I was sent to the principal's office and got licks with his paddle for the first time in first grade. It was an omen of things to come. Another kid and I were sticking our big first grade pencils in our ears, blunt end first of course. The teacher made us go stand in the hall. If you disrupted class in those days, you were made to go stand in the hall. Every now and then the principal would walk the two halls of the school to see if there were any troublemakers, scofflaws or ne'er do wells standing in the hall. He would then take you to his office to deal with the situation, which for boys pretty much meant a paddling.

Our principal was a tall man with thinning black hair and big bug eyes. He wore thick glasses and blinked all the time, forever earning the nickname "Frog Eyes" from every kid who ever went to school there. You could hear his wingtips squeaking and see his shadow as he was about to round the corner and head down the hall to confront you. He had a paddle with "Board of Education" painted on it hanging on the wall of his office. Sometimes you were lucky and stood in the hall for what seemed like an eternity and Frog Eyes never showed up. On this particular day we were not so fortunate. On the way to Frog Eyes' office, the other kid was screaming and crying the whole way, begging him to let us go. I remained stoic and brave and took my medicine like a little man. We went back to class and I never stuck another pencil in my ear, at least not in class. Corporal punishment had served its purpose.

In the third grade I saw a girl for the first time. I mean I really saw a girl. It was the first day of school and she walked in and sat down at the desk next to me. I looked at her and something in my eight year old brain clicked. I immediately realized that I didn't want to pull her hair and that she definitely did not have cooties. I'm not going to say who she was because we are still friends and I don't want to embarrass her. But she was every bit the Southern Belle then that she is today.

Then, like many other eight year olds before me and since, I fell in love with my third grade teacher. She was blonde, probably about twenty three or twenty four years old. She had a baritone ukulele and would play folk songs for us. *Where Have All The Flowers Gone*, *Michael Row The Boat Ashore*, *If I Had A Hammer*, *Puff The Magic Dragon*, *Lemon Tree* and *There Was A Crooked Man* are the ones that come to mind. She was obviously a Peter, Paul and Mary fan. I wrote her a note telling her she was my favorite teacher ever and convinced my mother to let me buy her a Christmas present. It was a costume jewelry brooch of Rudolph

The Red Nosed Reindeer.

The day that President Kennedy was assassinated, the Principal came over the loudspeakers in the classrooms and broke the news. A girl with flaming red hair that sat behind me started to cry. No one said a word and after a while the Principal came to the door and announced that our parents had been contacted and that school would be letting out early. The teacher sat at her desk and sobbed softly. She only taught the one year at Gresham Park.

In the fourth grade there was a girl that used to wink at me from across the room. She had dark hair and big brown eyes. I was a nine year old boy and a girl winking at me from across the room made me very uncomfortable. I was afraid one of my friends might see her. After the fourth grade she moved away and grew up to become Homecoming Queen at Gordon High. She was absolutely drop dead gorgeous. She worked in the dime store and drove a little chartreuse green VW. I was seventeen years old and would go into the store and buy jacks, rubber balls, a kazoo and a few marbles just to go through the check out line and gawk at her. I wanted to tell her that I liked her car and ask her if she remembered winking at me in the fourth grade, but my tongue would suddenly become the thickness of a slab of beef liver. All I could get out was "Hah… lahhhhk yur cahhhhhhhh".

There was another girl in my class that my father was

absolutely gaga over. She had long black hair that she wore in braids. My friend Herb's dad told me, "If I was your age, every time her momma threw dish water out the back door she'd hit me in the head." I never really understood what he meant until later. All I could picture was her mother stepping out the back door and dumping a bucket of water on my head.

By the end of the seventh grade and on the cusp of the teenage years, I had lost all interest in the Boy Scouts, Batman and the Popeye Club. All I cared about were girls and football. Looking back, the girls were much more mature at that age than most of my colleagues and I. For the most part, we were just trying to figure out what was going on.

The PTA rented Clifton Springs before our seventh grade graduation and threw us a big party. There was a lot of boyfriend and girlfriend drama going on. In pre-dating back then you "liked" somebody. So it was, "So and so has been liking so and so all year but he broke up with her and now he's over there on the beach with so and so. I can't believe he's liking her now."

I wasn't any part of that but one thing happened at that party that I will never forget as long as I live. There was a group of us boys in the jukebox room and a girl came in wearing her bikini and started dancing to Elvis's *U.S. Male*. She was shaking things I didn't know could be shook. I stood there with my jaw on the ground like

Wile. E. Coyote after the Road Runner had just smoked him. I had never seen a girl move like that in my life. I never would again. The memories are there. They always will be.

The Plaza

The Plaza was the heart of retail commerce in Gresham
Park. Its given name was Gresham Park Plaza but no
one ever called it that. It was known as the shopping
center or simply the store.

"Momma, can I go up to the store?" would be the first
words out of my mouth after I washed the car or cut
the grass for a dollar. A kid could go a long way at the
store with a dollar. Gresham Park Pharmacy was located
at the center of the plaza. It was known simply as the
drug store. It had a lunch counter where you could get
sandwiches, milk shakes and real cherry Cokes. Next
to the drug store was a Sears pickup store. This was
the predecessor of online shopping. You could order
things out of the Sears and Roebuck catalog and pick it
up the next day at the store in the shopping center. In
mid-twentieth century suburbia, this was the pinnacle
of convenience. Ace Hardware was next to Sears.
Gresham Park Barber Shop, where I got many a flat top
haircut, was next to the hardware store and next to that
was Gresham Park Beauty Salon. Next to the salon was
a shoe repair store where you could get taps put on your
shoes for a quarter. Then there was a gift shop where
I got my first Surfer's Cross necklace and bought my
third grade teacher's Rudolf The Red Nose Reindeer
costume jewelry brooch for Christmas. Finally there
was Gresham Park Cleaners, who sponsored my Little

League baseball team.

In the opposite direction from the drug store was Richard's Bargain City, better known as the dime store. A juvenile retail paradise, the dime store carried anything and everything a kid could possibly want. I bought countless car, airplane, monster and Weird-Oh plastic models there. Virtually all of our back to school supplies came from the dime store. There were board games, toys and sporting goods as well. You name it and the dime store had it. In the summer there was a big barrel of baseballs next to the door. Each one cost a dime. After being hit around the backyard for an afternoon your new dime store baseball would have the same basic shape and density as an orange.

The cash registers at the dime store were set up like the ones in the grocery store, with a conveyor and shelves containing point of purchase items. A petite redhead about three years older than me worked the register. I purchased many tubes of plastic model glue, bottles of paint, packs of notebook paper and soon-to-be-lumpy baseballs from her, never dreaming that one day we would become very close friends. Her mom worked in the store too.

Next to the dime store was Pilgrim's Cleaners, which featured a big neon sign depicting a pilgrim advertising ten cent washing and drying. Lastly there was the A&P grocery store. I had my picture made in the A&P when I was about twelve. It is a black and white portrait that we still have. The camera and backdrop were set up right there in the middle of the store.

A Big Apple grocery store opened at the south end of the plaza sometime in the Sixties. The dime store moved into a bigger space next to Big Apple and a haberdashery moved into its space next to the drug store. In a separate building across from the dime store was a pizza place. It then became a hot dog stand and eventually a printing company.

Last and most certainly not least was the convenience store located at the south entrance to the shopping center. It went through a number of different names but the store itself never changed. There was a bug zapper outside the door that was about the same size and wattage as a Georgia Power transformer. I remember stopping there at night and waiting in the car with my mother while my father went inside for a pack of Lucky Strikes. I was mesmerized by the bug zapper. It had a soft blue glow to it and there was a constant "Zzzzzt, Zzzzzt, Zzzzzt" from its hapless victims. Occasionally there would be a loud and prolonged "ZZZZZZZZZTTTTTTTTTT" accompanied by smoke as a large flying insect of some sort met its fate.

The convenience store was where we would go for bubble gum, candy, baseball cards and a frozen concoction known as The Slurpee. The Slurpee was blended frozen flavored ice dispensed from a machine into paper cups. It was The Holy Grail of Refreshments. Three sizes were available. You could get a small for a dime, a medium for a quarter and a large for the then astronomical sum of fifty cents. The flavors included cherry, cola and a variety of novelty flavors. I always liked the cola flavor. There was nothing better than a cola Slurpee after cutting the grass and riding your bike or walking to the store on a hot summer day. Right inside the front door of the store was a big bin of posters. They were rolled up in fine tubes and packaged in plastic. The posters were sorted by numbers and on the back of the bin there were small pictures of them with the appropriate bin number. I got my first posters there. Both were of Raquel Welch. One was the iconic black and white photo of her in the fur bikini from the movie "One Million Years B.C." The second was a color shot of her on the beach in a yellow bikini, stretching her arms over her head. Like pretty much every other pre-pubescent boy in the Sixties, I had a crush on Raquel Welch. Especially when she was wearing a bikini.

We rode our bikes or walked to the store all the time. There was a shortcut at the top of my street through a side yard and across a back yard. You had to run through the back yard because the rumor was that the man who lived there hated kids. He supposedly had a mean dog and would shoot at you if he saw you. I went through the side gate, sprinted across the back yard and jumped over the fence many times and no one ever even yelled at me or took a shot at me. Over time I figured that it was okay to cut through but I still sprinted as opposed to strolled. It was better to be safe than sorry.

We would stop at the gas stations as well to check the air in the tires of our bikes and ask for STP stickers. Mr. Brown owned the Standard station and was a kindly man. He would give us a sheet that had a large STP sticker in the middle and two small ones at the top left and right corners. We would plaster these on our bike seats and frames. I had a large STP sticker on the back of my go-kart's seat frame.

After one trip to the store my friend Billy and I rode our bikes over to the Sinclair Station on Brannen Road for a tire check before heading home. I decided that my front tire needed air, so I stuck the hose on the valve and hit the pump lever. The tire did not need air. The tube burst with a loud pop and the tire went as flat as a flitter. The service station man let me use the phone to call my father and he came to pick us up in his truck. I left my bike at the station to have the tire fixed and had to pay for the repair with my own money. That was when I learned to use a tire gauge.

I would ride to the grocery store with my mother and often would wait in the car while she went inside and shopped. Parents could do that back then. We had a '65 Ford Fairlane Sport Coupe. I would climb over the console to the driver's seat, buckle the lap belt and pretend that I was flying a plane all over the world. That was fun but it couldn't compare to when she would take the car to the Standard station for Mr. Brown to change the oil. He would let me sit in the driver's seat while he raised the car on the lift. You could do that back then too. The world was a lot better before litigation. I would be at the roof of the service bay flying high before coming in for a perfect three point landing as the lift lowered. I would then taxi over to the hangar at Gresham Park Airport while Momma paid Mr. Brown for the oil change. I would climb back over the console to the passenger's seat and she would drive us home. The memories are there. They always will be.

The Woods

In between our house and Bubba-Bubba's was a large patch of woods that was about twenty five square acres. There were two trails into the woods from our house. The top trail was accessed from the front left corner of the garage. I would cross the small lot on our property, go past my old swing set with the rocket ship and follow the trail through the briar patch and into the woods. The bottom trail was accessed by crossing our back yard, then down the hill to the creek and following it left into the woods. The trails were there for as long as I can remember. I assume that they were formed from years of routine use. I certainly did my part to help wear them down. They were the only trails that were on our side of the woods.

To us neighborhood kids, the woods may as well have been a forest. We went exploring there, camped out, caught crawfish and salamanders in the creek, shot our BB guns and played army. One of the first memories I have of Gresham Park was going into the woods with Billy and his older brother. Some of the older boys in the neighborhood were building a tree house. Years later Billy and I dug a huge hole in the ground just off of the top trail. We then covered the top of the hole and had an underground bunker. It was great until the first hard rain filled it with water. After it dried out, we took the top off and it became a foxhole during our military maneuvers.

I read a lot of outdoor adventure novels while in grammar school, *White Fang*, *The Call of the Wild* and *Old Yeller*, to name a few. But my favorite was *Big Red*, the story of a champion Irish Setter and a young trapper named Danny. There was a copy on the shelf in our school library. I checked it out at least once every year. I would read the story of the boy and the dog and envision myself in the wilds of the forest, hunting and exploring with my big red dog at my side. When school would let out in the afternoon I would ride my bike home, change clothes, strap my Boy Scout hatchet and knife to my belt, grab my Daisy BB gun and head for the woods. I would walk out of our back door and follow the lower trail along the creek all the way to the drain pipe that ran under the street at the bottom of the hill. I would then climb the hill going east and walk the ridge back to the creek behind our house. Sometimes I would climb the hill first and walk the eastern ridge down to where it overlooked the flood plain next to Bubba-Bubba's house. Then I would go down the hill and walk the trail along the creek. Or, I would take the top trail that led from the entrance at the left of our house and wound to the right along the top of the western ridge past our big foxhole and follow the trail down the hill to the creek. I would spend at least an hour in the woods on the weekdays after school, usually by myself. I longed to be exploring the woods with my Irish Setter sniffing out chipmunks, treeing squirrels and flushing out flocks of blue jays. My parents would not hear of an Irish Setter, due to the fact that we already had a Boston Terrier named Bozo. He was a good dog and I loved him, but he was not a hunting, tracking or retrieving dog. Besides, he had a propensity to run off, so if I had taken him to the woods I would've spent the afternoon chasing a runaway Boston Terrier through various neighborhoods.

Saturdays were the days we played Army. Many different operations were carried out and battles were waged in the woods after Saturday morning cartoons. We all had our Army uniforms, helmets and combat boots from the army surplus store in East Atlanta. I had a tommy gun that went rat-a-tat-tat-tat-tat when you pulled back the lever on the side and held onto the trigger. Billy had an old Daisy air rifle that had the mechanism taken out. When he cocked the lever and pulled the trigger the gun gave off a loud bang. Brain had a Winchester lever action carbine that used Greenie Stick 'Em caps and shot plastic bullets. A couple of other kids had similar weapons as well. We actually shot at each other with these. The rules were you couldn't aim at anybody's head, only the body. Safety was paramount in Saturday Morning Warfare. If you got hit in the chest, you were out and had to lie down and play dead. If you got hit in the arm or leg, you were wounded. You could still shoot, but you could not move from that spot. We had battery powered walkie-talkies to communicate with and plastic hand grenades with Stick 'Em caps that exploded when they hit the ground after you tossed them. If a grenade landed next to you and the cap went off, you were out. If the cap didn't go off, the grenade was a dud and you fought on.

One of our favorite games was Capture The Flag. We would play with both armies on either side of the creek. Sometimes other kids from other neighborhoods would come in and we would have a battle royal that might last all afternoon. Other times we would all team up and fight an imaginary enemy. We would usually start at the creek behind my house, advance up the hill and take the Huns that were at the top of my back yard. We always emerged victorious in these battles. The imaginary enemy never won.

Anna lived across the street. She had an older brother who used to throw the baseball with me in their front yard. Anna and I played together all the time. She loved animals and was not squeamish about bugs, lizards or any other creepy crawly things. One day she and I went to the woods and played in the creek. We turned over rocks and caught crawfish. She found a few pieces of quartz for her rock collection. That evening when I went home, I told my mother Anna and I had played in the creek in the woods. She looked at me sternly and said that I couldn't go play in the woods with Anna again. "Why not?" I asked.

"Oh, you can never go into the woods with a girl."

"How come?"

"It's not right."

"What's not right about it?"

"You just can't go into the woods with a girl. Period."

That was all the explanation I got. I didn't understand what was wrong with catching crawfish in the creek with Anna. I still don't.

The creek that ran through the woods was a tributary of Sugar Creek. It was small, only about a foot or so deep. It may have dipped down to two feet in spots. It was perfect for exploring, building dams, turning over stones, catching crawfish and salamanders, hunting for fossils, collecting rocks and getting water when we were camping.

We camped in the woods all the time. We would pitch our tents by the creek and build a small fire to cook hot dogs and roast marshmallows. We would stay up at night telling ghost stories and reading Mad magazines by flashlight. If we were feeling brave and adventurous we would go exploring. When I was in the Boy Scouts, one of the requirements for a camping merit badge was a two night camping trip alone. I went to the woods to do mine. On Friday afternoon I pitched my tent and laid out my sleeping bag inside of it. I dug my latrine, which I covered up before I left. I gathered rocks for my fireplace and wood for my fire. My father had let me borrow his fishing cooler and that is where I kept my food. I had my hatchet and my knife for chopping and whittling. I also had my BB gun with me in case any wild animals showed up. I stayed there Friday afternoon and Friday night, all day Saturday and Saturday night, and finally went back home on Sunday evening. Billy and Brain came by on Saturday to visit and my adult counselor for the merit badge came by each day to check on me. I was genuinely sad to see the weekend come to an end and I earned the merit badge with ease.

The last time I camped in the woods was when I was fifteen years old. My buddy Moon and I camped out one Saturday night. One of the older guys from Moon's neighborhood bought us a six-pack of tall boy Schlitz beer. We drank three apiece and wound up climbing trees.

Right before we moved from Gresham Park, I went into the woods one afternoon and sat high up on the eastern ridge. I hadn't spent much time in the woods during the last few years that we had lived there. Those days were gone, replaced by cars, girls and football. But that day the memories flooded back, of playing army, catching crawfish and exploring the trails and ridges. I sat there looking down at the creek. It gurgled and babbled and the blue jays, which had always filled the woods for as long as I could remember, were calling and squawking. I sat there for a long time before I got up and went home.

I never went in the woods again. But that day as I sat high on the eastern ridge, the memories were there. They always will be.

Bikes, Boards and Coaster Wagons

Rollingwood Lane was great for going down the hill on a bicycle until you hit a pothole and flew over the handlebars like I did as a nine year old. My bike was an appropriately named Sears Flight Liner and I was coming down the hill on it alongside one of the kids who lived up the street. I remember the front of the bike starting to shake and the next thing I knew I was staggering around and crying in Billy's yard across the street from our house. Apparently I had gone over the front of the Flight Liner and down the street on my chin. My father came running out of the door of our house, scooped me up and took me to see Aunt Hurricane. The other kid was coming down the street pushing his bike and carrying mine. The front wheel of the Flight Liner was mangled and bent. He was wearing my baseball cap on top of his and he looked terrified.

Aunt Hurricane was the local pediatrician. She got her name from her days playing semi-pro softball on a barnstorming softball team known as the Lorelei Ladies. As a doctor she stitched up, patched and cared for many an injured or sick Gresham Park Kid. She was boisterous and funny and had a wonderful manner with children. No matter how banged up you were or how poorly you felt, Aunt Hurricane always made you laugh and feel better.

She soothed and bandaged my wounds, gave me a hug, a kiss and a card for a free ice cream cone at the drug store. When I went to school on Monday I had to ease gingerly into the seat at my desk. The Girl sat next to me. I must've looked pretty scary because she looked at me in wide eyed wonder and asked what in the world had happened to me. "I flew over the handlebars of my bicycle and went down the street on my chin," I said. Years later she told me that the way that I looked had frightened her so that she never learned to ride a bicycle. Great. Not only was she the first girl that I had ever really seen but I had also traumatized her for life.

My wounds healed and before long I was back on the street riding my new orange Schwinn Stingray bike with a banana seat and high handlebars. The Flight Liner was relegated to a corner of the basement, bent wheel and all. I modified it in the seventh grade by putting a twenty inch wheel on the back and a new twenty six inch wheel on the front. It looked cool and rode like a chopper.

To challenge the hill we built a lot of stuff ourselves. Like skateboards, for instance. My first and only skateboard was a board that I cut out on my father's band saw. I shaped it like a surfboard, sanded it down and painted it white. I then painted a red racing stripe down the middle and topped it off with a big decal of Rat Fink in the center. I varnished it to protect the paint and Rat Fink. I let it dry overnight. The next morning I took the wheels off of an old roller skate and mounted them on the bottom. Cowabunga, Surf City!

We also built a lot of coaster wagons. They were the kind with a long, wide board for the body, a stationary axle bolted at the back, a front axle with a single bolt for an axis and a rope nailed onto each end of the axle for steering. Two boards were nailed on the body for a seat and one for a footrest. Lawnmower wheels were bolted onto the axles and a board was bolted onto the side for a brake. Billy and I built one following this plan. We saved our grass cutting and car washing money and rode our bikes to the hardware store to buy the bolts, nuts and washers for the axles and wheels. The boards were used from scrap lumber lying around our fathers' garages. If something broke on the wagon we could fix it ourselves. It was simple engineering at its finest. For years, we rode the coaster down the hill and pulled it back up.

I also built a scooter that looked like a Honda motorcycle. It had a frame with a stand and a wooden seat on it. I put a stand on the front as well and bolted an old pair of bicycle handlebars onto it. I took the wheels off of another pair of old roller skates and mounted them on the bottom at the front and the back. I painted the scooter red and white, put a V-rroom motor on it and had myself a homemade Honda.

Billy also built his own skateboard. We helped some of the other kids in the neighborhood build their skateboards and coaster wagons too. We would race from Brain's driveway to the two storm drains on opposite sides of the street at the bottom of the hill. We rode anything we could down the hill, from Radio Flyer wagons to Flexy Racers to Brain's kid brother's Big Wheel. There were a number of wipeouts and crackups but no major injuries. The biggest mishap came when we took to riding our bicycles through the paths in the woods along Sugar Creek. Billy was riding barefoot one Saturday morning and one of his toes got caught in a vine. It yanked all the skin off and almost took the toe with it. After a trip to see Aunt Hurricane he was fine, but his toe looked like a Vienna sausage.

After we outgrew the old coaster wagon it stayed propped up on one side in a corner of the garage. My father suffered a heart attack when I was fifteen years old. While he was recovering and not long before he went back to work he began to work on projects around the house. One day when I arrived home from school he said, "Come on downstairs, I've got something to show you." We walked down into the basement and sitting there in the middle of the garage floor was the old coaster wagon. It had been drastically modified. He had put a wide seat of plywood on the bottom frame and built an outhouse around it, complete with a half moon on either side so that you could see out. It was open in the front with a footrest horizontally across the frame and it still had the original steering rope. It looked just like Huey's Hut Rod from the old Weird-Oh model kits we used to build not too many years before. "I started working," he said, "and this is what happened." Even though we were fifteen and had outgrown such toys we rode the Hut Rod down the street all the time. The only problem was that the Hut Rod was a little top heavy. Once while trying to show off I made a hard left turn at the bottom of the hill and turned over on the side. I scrambled out and managed to get it upright before a bus came barreling down the hill.

I took a picture of the Hut Rod parked out in the driveway. It was taped to the door of the big cabinet in my father's workshop for years. I don't know what became of the Hut Rod or the picture, but I have my suspicions. Whatever happened, the picture is gone now as is the Hut Rod and the cabinet. But the memories are there. They always will be.

Backyard Ball

Besides playing organized sports, we played a lot of backyard ball. And that's literally what it was. Basketball was played in Billy's back yard. He had a Sears backboard and goal bolted to a big oak tree. The rim was set at ten feet. There was no adjustable pole, so as youngsters we had to try and hit the basket at regulation height just like the older kids. The tree with the goal was in front of the eight foot chain link fence at the back of Billy's yard. That part of the yard was level. It was hard packed dirt from years of backyard ball. Kids came from all around to Billy's backyard basketball court. We would play games of horse for hours on end. The game of horse is played with two or more people. Players begin the game by shooting from the foul line. Our foul line was a rut in the dirt. We only used it for games of horse since there were no foul shots in our regular games. The first person to make a basket then can take any kind of shot from anywhere. If that person makes the basket, the next person has to attempt to make the same shot. If the shot is missed, that person is awarded the letter "h". The game continues on with the letters "o", "r" and so on. The first person to spell out "horse" is out of the game. The last one standing wins.

In our regular games the first team to twenty points was the winner. We would play basketball year round in all kinds of weather except snow, when we would engage in snowball fights. Billy's family moved when we were fifteen and he gave me the basketball goal. I put it on a big tree in our side yard. I shot some hoops on it every now and then, but it was never the same. No kids came around and I eventually began to play in the pickup games in the gym at the ballpark. I left the goal on the tree when we moved from Gresham Park.

Our baseball field was also in Billy's back yard. First base was the tree with the basketball goal and second base was the post on the low split rail fence between Billy and Brain's back yards. Third base was a rock placed on the ground across from the tree with the basketball goal. Home was a piece of plywood cut in the shape of home plate and periodically painted white. It was in front of the six foot wooden fence, which also served as our backstop. The pitching rubber was a tree root in the middle of the yard and the outfield was Brain's back yard across the split rail fence. It was makeshift, but it was ours and it worked.

The football field was Bubba-Bubba's side yard. It was a large flood plain from the creek that ran through the woods and was a perfect football field. We played many a game there and often against kids from other streets and neighborhoods. At the end of the field next to the street were two trees about ten feet apart. They had two limbs that crossed and this was our goal post. When a team scored, we lined up with the rock that marked the goal line and attempted the extra point. There was no snap and hold. We used a tee and the defensive team would rush and attempt to block the kick. If a team that was going in the opposite direction decided to kick a field goal, they would set up at the same yardage facing the trees.

We played tackle. There was no two hand touch below the waist and no pads. Every once in a while someone would get a black eye or a bloody nose. There would be an inevitable shoving match, but there were no fights. No kid ever ran home crying and most certainly nobody's mother came and took them off the field and out of the game.

Backyard ball didn't end with the coming of adolescence. We shot hoops and threw the baseball and football around Billy's yard up until he moved away. I don't remember the last time we played football at Bubba-Bubba's, but the games had pretty much ended there by the time Billy left. By that time we had moved to bigger games on bigger fields.

In high school and beyond, there were pickup football games everywhere. There was always a game going on at Gresham Park, as well as Bouldercrest Park in Cedar Grove and Exchange Park at Southwest DeKalb. Sometimes we would even climb over the fence and play at Panthersville Stadium. My buddy Moon would call me up on a Saturday or Sunday morning and ask, "You want to play today?"

"Sure. You got a game?"

"Nah, we'll find one."

I would drive up to his house and we would hit the ballparks and apartment complexes until we found a game.

One day we were playing at Exchange Park and were deciding who was going to kick off and who was going to receive. A guy named Big Mike asked one of the Sharp Brothers to pick a number between one and ten. "Seven," said the Sharp Brother. "Nah, that's not it. We'll receive," said Big Mike. The Sharp Brothers team kicked off. A few plays later the Sharp Brother who had done the picking realized what had happened. "Hey, wait a minute! Who told you it was number seven?" he yelled at Big Mike. "Never mind, it doesn't matter now," said Big Mike. The Sharp Brothers were not the brightest crayons in the box and certainly did not live up to their name.

Later on in the same game Moon, who was a big guy himself, almost came to blows with Big Mike. Even though the two of them were good friends, on the field things can sometime become heated. I know you are supposed to stick by your buddy no matter what, but there was no way I was getting my one hundred and sixty five pound body in between those two behemoths. "I hate to say it, Moon, but you're on your own with this one," I told him in the huddle. Things cooled down like they always did and the two of them drank beer together after the game like nothing had ever happened.

It's a miracle that no one was seriously killed or maimed in those backyard games. It was full speed, full contact tackle football with no pads. We were pretty much fully grown, at least physically. A guy showed up at one of the games at Panthersville wearing a mouthpiece and was laughed off the field. I saw guys get knocked cold, but never saw an injury where an ambulance had to be summoned.

At Stone Mountain one Sunday afternoon, we pulled into the back parking lot and stationed ourselves on the front fender of Moon's Camaro. There was a big field across from the parking lot and a bunch of guys were playing football. We decided to go over and get in the game. They put me on one team and Moon on the other. I went out on the right corner and on the first play they ran a sweep to my side. I stepped into the ball carrier, put my shoulder into his waist, head to one side and took him down. I didn't hit him hard, just a textbook tackle. The guy came up swinging and cursing. "Hey, you blankity-blank, we're playing touch!" he yelled. Moon and I looked at each other and sneered. After a few more plays we looked at each other again and said, "Forget this." We went back across the street to the parking lot, drank beer and chatted up girls.

Moon blew out his knee in a game at the old Forest Park stadium. We started out late on a Sunday and wound up finding a game there. Once again, we were put on opposite teams. At one point Moon's team had the ball. They completed a pass, gained about ten yards and the receiver was tackled. The play was over. Moon was standing next to the guy on the ground who had caught the ball. Out of the blue some little guy ran up and for no apparent reason hit Moon's left knee. It was a cheap shot. Moon went down and came back up grimacing in pain and limping badly. That was it for us. But before we left, Moon stuck his finger in the guy's chest and said, "I've got to leave now, but I'm looking at your face. I've got a real good memory and if I ever see you again, I'm going to kick your [backside]." The guy had a look of absolute terror on his face. Moon had knee surgery and his backyard ball career was over. Luckily for the guy, Moon never saw him again. If he had, I would have known it and probably would have been somehow involved.

I continued to play up into my late twenties at Glenwood Hills in a league that I found advertised on a flyer in Manuel's Tavern. The last year that I played our team joined a flag league at Hammond Park in Sandy Springs. We went 10-0 and won the championship. I hated it. No contact was allowed, period. If you can't hit and be hit, it's not football. I'm sorry, but that's the way I feel.

I've always said that I'd like to suit up in my old jersey and sweats one more time for a round of backyard ball. Birthdays have made that impossible now. I wouldn't be able to walk for a month. But the memories are there. They always will be.

The Madison

The Madison Theatre was the closest movie theatre to Gresham Park. It was located on Flat Shoals Avenue in the heart of East Atlanta. The building, though derelict and empty, is still standing.

The old theatre opened in July of 1927. It was, according to an opening day press clipping, "considered to be the last word in small-theatre construction and furnishing, incorporating all the features which are found in the most modern downtown theatre."

The Madison must have indeed been grand. On the outside, the facade resembled the gothic designs of the day. Inside, the balcony featured large windows that could be opened. There was a "cry room" where parents could take noisy children. It had a large glass window in the front so that those inside could view the show. The sound was piped in through speakers. Teenagers used the cry room for other purposes in later years. Out of curiosity I ventured into it once as a kid. I was promptly told to get out.

Forty years later, the Madison had lost most of its original grandeur. By the mid-Sixties the carpet was sticky and gooey, undoubtedly from having decades worth of soft drinks, buttered popcorn, candy and Lord knows what else spilled on it. The seats were worn and the bathrooms were dirty, but the one thing that had not left the Madison was fun and entertainment.

The first movie I ever saw was at the Madison. My mother took me to see *The Shaggy Dog.* I don't remember much about it, but my mother said it scared me when Tommy Kirk started turning into a dog. That was when I was about five. A few years later I went with my older cousins to see *The Creature From The Black Lagoon.* It scared me to death as well. The only difference was that after the movie I went next door to Forrest 5&10 and bought a plastic model of the Creature. I became a certified movie buff and as far as I was concerned, the Madison was the only theatre in town.

I would earn a dollar by washing the car or cutting the grass. My mother would take either my cousin or one of the neighborhood kids and me to the Madison and drop us off. There were often double features. You could stay all day and watch the movies over and over. If you arrived in the middle of a movie, you could watch it and then sit through it again until you got to the point where you came in. A single admission for a quarter covered it all. You could get a Coke for a dime and a candy bar for a nickel. You could also get asphyxiated in the lobby from all of the hoods hanging around in there smoking. I don't think they came to the Madison to watch movies at all. I think they were there just to hang around in the lobby and smoke. Maybe it was a turf thing.

Some of the movies I saw at the Madison were *The Blob,*

Cat Ballou, A Hard Days Night, Help, Frankenstein, Wolfman, Godzilla, Goldfinger, Thunder Road and *Your Cheatin' Heart*. Out of all the monsters, Godzilla was by far my favorite. There was also a movie called *The Legend Of Blood Mountain*, which starred Atlanta TV personality Bestoink Dooley. It was filmed at Stone Mountain. The monster was wrapped in what appeared to be gauze and wearing a Halloween mask. In the end, Bestoink killed the monster with a flamethrower and it rolled down the side of Stone Mountain in a ball of fire.

In 1963 my aunt took my cousin and me to the Madison to see a movie that would change my life. The movie was *It Happened At The World's Fair* starring Elvis Presley. I was hooked. After that, I saw probably every movie that Elvis ever made and saw them all at the Madison. They would show them when they were fresh out of Hollywood and the older ones as re-runs. I thought Elvis was the coolest thing on the face of the earth. He could ride down the road on a motorcycle and his hair would stay perfectly in place. He would then burst into song accompanied by a full band, presumably in his saddlebags. He would always wind up with the pretty girl. It was a formula that worked. It certainly worked on me. I wanted to grow up and be just like Elvis, only I wanted to be an astronaut. I figured that they could make a movie of me blasting off, singing in space, saving the world and then splashing down and marrying the pretty girl.

My cousins' grandparents owned a little restaurant up the street from The Madison called The Yum-Yum. My aunt worked there. We would walk up to the Yum-Yum after the movies for a hot dog or a hamburger and a Coke. My father worked at the fire station a few doors up and across the street from The Yum-Yum. Sometimes we would walk there to see him. My aunt or my mother would then pick us up and take us home.

I'm not sure exactly when the Madison closed. The last movie I saw there was in '68. Fittingly, it was *Speedway* starring Elvis and Nancy Sinatra. Same formula. Elvis played a stock car driver whose manager gambled away all his money and landed him in hot water with The Taxman. Nancy was the beautiful IRS agent assigned to monitor Elvis's winnings on the track. They fell in love and everyone lived happily ever after. If it ain't broke, don't fix it.

The Madison fell into disrepair. It was a furniture storage place for a while, but has now sat boarded up and empty for years. That is a shame. Forrest 5&10 next door burned to the ground sometime in the Seventies, but the fire did not damage the structure of the old theatre. It is hard to believe that someone has not bought the property and restored it. It would be a perfect venue for a restaurant, concert hall or theatre. Instead, the Madison sits there, boarded up, rotting and for rent. But the memories are there. They always will be.

Trick Or Treat

Trick or Treat was always a big time in Gresham Park. I'm sure that Richard's 5&10 made a fortune selling Halloween costumes. They were simple, one piece nylon outfits that buttoned or zipped up at the back and a plastic mask with two eye holes and an elastic band that held it on your head. Some of the choices were a witch, a devil, a skeleton, a princess, a pirate, a hobo, Frankenstein, Wolfman, Dracula, Wonder Woman, The Lone Ranger and Casper The Friendly Ghost. I refuse to even mention a clown. Clowns scared me then and give me the heebie jeebies now.

While the costumes from the store were all well and good, the best were the ones that were homemade. One year a girl from the next street over came out wearing a cardboard box over her shoulders with her head sticking out of a hole cut in the top. The box was made up like a dinner table complete with a tablecloth, paper plates, plastic knives, forks, spoons and paper cups. There was a sign on the front that said, "I'm The Head Of The Table." If there had been a prize for best neighborhood costume she would have won hands down.

The Halloween night that I remember most was with a friend of mine from school. He lived in a one street neighborhood that was not at all conducive to Trick or Treating. I invited him to go with me in our neighborhood. We started out right before dark. All of the kids in the neighborhood were in groups of two, four or six. There were no adults with any of us. There was no need. Besides, the parents had to stay home and distribute the treats. The two of us went all the way up Rollingwood on one side and came back down on the other. After stopping at my house to empty our Trick or Treat bags, we set out again and moved over to the other streets in the neighborhood. We visited the doorsteps of the houses on Boulderview, which crossed Rollingwood at the top and then headed down Hidden Forest Court, which ran off of Boulderview to the right.

A lady who lived at the corner of Hidden Forest and Boulderview invited us inside when we knocked on her door. There was a group of kids in there already. Remember, it was a different time and place back then. She put us all in a circle and we sang *Three Little Fishes* as a round. Then she pulled out a big tray of candied apples, fudge and brownies. We each got our pick of one and continued on our way.

Another mom in the neighborhood dressed up like a witch and scared the wits out of us when she opened the door. We got our candy and left as quickly as we could, convinced that she was going to mount her broom and chase us out of the yard and up the street.

My mother would make candied apples as well, both plain and dipped in melted caramel. I would always hope that there would be a couple of them left over by the end of the night. The trays would be empty when I finally got home. Then she would pull out one each of the candied and caramel apples that she had saved for me. That night she saved two of each for my friend and for me.

Like the costumes, the best treats were homemade. Besides candied apples there was fudge, brownies, Rice Krispie treats and those wonderful caramel popcorn balls held together with melted marshmallows. They were about the size of a softball and biting into one was Trick Or Treat Nirvana.

There was never any mischief either. I don't remember any carloads of hooligans riding around throwing eggs or firecrackers. About the worst I ever heard of was a house that somebody said a teenage kid would put ice in your bag and tell you that it was rock candy. He would then follow you from a distance. When the ice started to melt and the bottom of your paper Trick Or Treat bag fell apart, he would scoop up the treats that fell out of your bag. I'm sure that it never really happened. There was only one house that gave out homemade rock candy. Brain's mom made it and she always tied it up in a little plastic bag.

I only remember two of the costumes that I wore on Halloween. One was my Robin outfit that my mother made for me in the middle of the Batman craze. The

second was when I was twelve years old. We had
traveled to Texas to see my new little niece who had
been born in August. We got back home about nine
o'clock on Halloween night. I put on my long, dark
green cloth raincoat, my black leather gloves, my
father's fedora and the mask from my Robin outfit. I
was The Green Hornet. I went around to four or five
houses close to ours. I was the only kid on the street and
that was the last time I ever went Trick Or Treating. The
memories are there. They always will be.

A White Christmas, Almost

When I was nine years old, I got a sled for Christmas. It was a beautiful, brand new Flexible Flyer. In some parts of the world a kid's first sled is a rite of passage, like learning to ride a bike without training wheels, losing your first tooth or getting your first BB gun. But for a kid growing up in Georgia, a sled was a bit of a stretch.

As it turned out, Santa Claus must have been tuned into the weather reports and known exactly what was coming. The year was 1964 and it snowed on New Year's Day. Christmas vacation was extended for a few days and the snow on the ground was a perfect consistency of powder and ice.

The cold wasn't bitter enough to keep us from going outside. We didn't care anyway. We were kids. We went outside and played in the snow. After a few hours, I would go home and take my galoshes off at the front door. Then I would go inside, sit down on the kitchen floor next to the furnace vent, take off my socks and warm my feet. After they were sufficiently thawed I would put on a couple pairs of fresh socks, pull on my galoshes and hit the powder again.

And my brand new Flexible Flyer was grand. I could start in our front yard, cross the driveway, hit the street and ride all the way to the bottom of the hill. Billy had a sled too and we would race, ride in pairs and swap off sleds. He showed me how to ride sitting up and to steer using my feet on the crossbar, as opposed to trying to steer it using the rope. The rope, he taught me, was simply for pulling the sled back up the hill. Billy's father was from upstate New York, so Billy was familiar with such matters.

Brain and his kid brother used a cut open cardboard box. When it started to fall apart they would cut up another one. The kids up the street were riding down the hill two to four at a time in a flat bottom fiberglass dinghy. The grown ups even got in on the fun. My father rode the Flexible Flyer down the hill a few times. He liked to go down head first, steering with his hands on the crossbar. A couple of times I went down the hill with him, riding on his back. Then I went down head first on my own. A safety helmet? Please. It was 1964.

We had snowball fights, our side of the street against theirs. They took place with their team on the hill in the Billy's front yard and our team in our front yard. They usually won due to the fact that we had to throw uphill. Billy's American bulldog Socko wandered around in the street, oblivious to the winter combat that was going on around him. He just lumbered up the hill amid a hail of snowball salvos, occasionally taking a hit to the rear end before lying down on his bed on the front porch for a nap.

Every family on the street built a Snowman or a Mr. and

Mrs. Snowman in their yard. My mother would make snow cones. She would come outside with paper cone cups and food coloring. We would make snowballs and she would put them in the cups and add the food coloring. It was as tasty as a Slurpee on a hot summer day.

Eventually the snow melted and went away. We returned to school from the Christmas holidays. The problem was that Snow '64 had left an indelible impression on my young mind. I thought that it was going to snow every year between Christmas and New Year's, the kind that we could play in for hours. I anxiously awaited the next winter wonderland like the one we had frolicked in before.

Christmas came. New Year's went. No snow. There was finally a light dusting sometime in January or February. I bundled up and ran out into the front yard. I hit the ground head first on the Flexible Flyer. It didn't budge and almost knocked the breath out of me. I tried sitting up on the sled and pushing. It still didn't budge. I moved out into the street and tried there. Flexible Flyers don't fly very well on slush and pavement. I eventually gave up and trudged back to the house. I took off my galoshes at the front door, went inside and warmed my feet over the vent. By the next day the snow was gone and I was older, wiser and greatly disappointed.

I don't remember riding the Flexible Flyer again or what

became of it. It hung on the wall in the garage for years, reduced to being nothing more than a mere ornament. But for one week of a young boy's life it was the perfect Christmas gift. The memories of the Flexible Flyer and the Almost White Christmas are there. They always will be.

Warhawks

On a spring day in 1968, we seventh graders were gathered in the lunchroom at Gresham Park Elementary School. The head counselor at Walker High School was there to speak to us. "Here you are a very big fish in a very small pond," he told us. "You are about to become a very small fish in a very big pond." He could not have been more right. Nothing in the world could have prepared us for what lay ahead.

We were on the cusp of graduating and would be attending high school in the fall. For most of us that high school would be Walker. All of our anticipation was about to become reality. We were ready to move past the juvenile world of elementary school and take advantage of the grown up things that we had heard about, such as being able to chew gum in class and to hold hands in the hall.

The previous seven years had been leading up to us becoming part of that institute of higher learning which included sports, clubs, beauty pageants, dances and specialized classes such as shop, home ec, art, typing, drafting and gym. A list of available classes had been handed out that day and one that caught my eye was "Small Gas Engine Repair." That sounded beyond cool. I decided then and there that I was going to take Small Gas Engine Repair.

I remember the first day of high school, walking through the doors and into the building that would become such a huge part of my life. It was like stepping into another world. I had never seen anything like it before. There was a sea of people and I was indeed a very small fish in a very big pond. The boys were all giants and the girls were all full blown women. I had never seen girls like that in school in my life. Couples walked by holding hands, so the rumor that we had heard was true.

Eighth grade classes were in blocs. That meant that we were divided into groups and moved from class to class together. Each bloc was a mix of students from different elementary schools in the area. We changed classes every hour. The required eighth grade courses were English, math, Georgia history, science and physical education or, as it was more commonly known, gym class. Gym was required in eighth and ninth grades. So, you only had one elective class and in the eighth grade the selection was pretty much limited to art, chorus or study hall. No shop, no home ec, no typing, no drafting and no small gas engine repair.

We went to lunch during third period while the rest of the school went during fourth. We had our own sports teams, to a certain extent. For the boys there was eighth grade football, basketball and, for some reason, track. Eighth grade girls' basketball started in the '69-70 school year. There was no softball program in the DeKalb

County school system at that time.

We had our own civic club, Jr. Civitan, Jr. We also had our own student council representatives and our own class Homecoming representative. We really were secluded and sheltered from the rest of the school. All of that ended after my eighth grade year. The bloc system was dropped and the eighth graders were funneled into the mainstream of the school curriculum.

By the ninth grade, you were just starting to get your sea legs. You were no longer on the bottom rung, but still pretty low on the food chain. By the tenth grade you were moving on up and beginning to gain recognition. The eleventh graders, or juniors, were part of the upper echelon and biding their time until the next school year. The seniors ruled the roost. The senior class defined the entire school year.

A huge part of Walker and her legacy were the cars. Those were the days when a racecar could basically be purchased right off of the showroom floor and Walker had more than its share of cool rides and bad beasts. Chevelles, Mustangs, Camaros, Chargers and Javelins, you name it and it was there. There were sports cars as well and a collection of VWs that would make Wolfsburg proud.

And there was Smoke City. Smoke City was called such because it evolved from a bunch of guys hanging out at the top of the student parking lot in the morning. They would stop drivers pulling into the lot in muscle cars and encourage them to light up the back tires. If a driver chose to do so, he had the option of the Smoke City Pit Crew pouring bleach on the pavement in front of the back wheels. This would cause the spinning tires to smoke even more. Someone even painted "Smoke City" in big white letters amid the tire marks at the top of the lot. The parking lot itself was a narrow strip less than a quarter mile long with a turnaround at the end. The spaces were marked on the side next to the school. Everybody backed into the spaces in the morning, because trying to back out of a space when everyone was leaving at the end of the school day was next to impossible. Others would parallel park along the opposite curb. As a result, the area of pavement between the two rows was very narrow. How a car was never hit from a Smoke City participant, I will never know.

Sports were a huge part of campus life. I played football all five years at Walker and loved every minute of it. We endured some tough seasons, but we were teammates, friends and we had a blast. The main sport at Walker was wrestling. We won the state championship five years in a row and numerous county and region titles as well. Walker also won the state baseball title, the boys' gymnastic title and the girls' tennis title.

The Royal Redcoat Marching Band was one of the

finest in the area. They worked very hard and often in very extreme conditions, practicing in the heat of the summer and the cold of the late fall and early winter. We could hear them on the baseball field as we practiced football on the field below. The bandleader was a very talented and passionate man. He used a bullhorn when he admonished his charges and I'm sure that he could be heard all the way up to East Atlanta.

During my eighth grade year, WSB Radio sponsored a "School Spirit" contest and Walker won. This was no doubt due to the cheerleaders. The cheerleaders were co-ed and worked with undying enthusiasm at both the pep rallies and the games. The pep rallies were a great part of school life and not only because you got out of sixth period class. They were social gatherings and a lot of fun. You yelled as loud as you could yell. The cheerleaders always put on skits and did cartwheels on the hardwood gym floor. On one occasion one of the girls fell and was knocked out cold.

The Royalettes were the drill team. They were elegant, precise and marched not only at the football games but in county, region and state competitions. They wore sequined, one piece outfits, as did the majorettes. The drill team's outfits were solid crimson or silver. The majorettes' were black and white or solid silver. I always felt for the girls when they performed in those outfits in freezing cold and wet November weather. I'm sure that on those nights the majorettes were glad to have been twirling fire batons.

Our mascot was Thor. Thor was a red-tailed hawk who lived in one of the school's courtyards. After he passed over to The Rainbow Bridge he was preserved, mounted and sat on the fence behind the cheerleaders during the football games. Otherwise he resided in the big glass trophy case in the gym lobby. Years later a group of alumni returned to the school to retrieve any WHS memorabilia they could find. The five wrestling state championship trophies were found in a closet. Thor had been painted orange and was being used as a doorstop. He was rescued, taken to a taxidermist and somehow cleaned and preserved. A display case was built for him and now our grand and noble mascot makes appearances at all of our reunions.

The three civic clubs were Kappa, Key and Jr. Civitan. Kappa was all girls, Key was all boys and Jr. Civitan was co-ed. I belonged to Jr. Civitan. The Civitan year culminated in a trip to Jekyll Island for the state convention. We all traveled together on a bus. Once there, the boys stayed in one hotel and the girls in another. I rode by the convention center and the hotel while on vacation at Jekyll years later. It brought back a lot of memories. There was a beauty pageant and a dance with a live band every night after the meetings. The Hastings Award winner, which was given to the top club in the state, was announced the final night of the convention. For a bunch of high school kids, it was literally a week at the beach.

Jr. Civitan put together a haunted house during my senior year to raise money for Civitan International. It was one of those things in a perfect place and time where everything came together. The whole thing was my buddy Moon's idea. He raised the proposal one night in our weekly meeting. A girl in the club mentioned that her grandmother owned a large house that was empty. It was located on the East Atlanta side of Flat Shoals Road. Her family gave us the okay and the Civitan Haunted House was on. The house was very large with two stories, an attic and a basement. It looked foreboding from the outside and was spooky on the inside. We approached local businesses about loaning us equipment for the house. Atlanta Costume Company provided all of the makeup. We advertised by posting flyers anywhere we could, but opening night was something that we were not expecting. People showed up in droves to tour the Haunted House. Dracula, Wolfman, Frankenstein, ghosts, witches and haints roamed about, mingling with the steady stream of frightened patrons that flowed through the house the entire night. Word of mouth spread and every night hundreds of visitors were sent through the house in shifts. I was the Dr. Frankenstein and my lab was in the basement. My assistant was a girl dressed up like Igor and one night I happened to hit her with an iron pipe, opening up a gash in her head. I was using the pipe to beat the monster back into submission and onto the table before he could grab the guests who were exiting the house from the basement door. After that I switched to a rubber hose. Years later, at one of our reunions, she pointed at the scar on her head and asked me, "Do you remember this?" I assured her that I did, that I still felt terrible about it and I apologized to her yet again.

Once a night, Moon and I would climb out of one of the attic windows and get into a "struggle" on the roof of the big front porch. Moon was Wolfman and was perfect for the part, which he played to the hilt. At one point during the struggle I would fall flat. Moon would pick up a dummy and throw it off of the roof and into the crowd below, eliciting screams and shrieks of terror.

One day we received word that WQXI's morning radio personality would be there that evening to tour the house. On the air the next morning he stated that he had been to all of the haunted houses in Atlanta and ours was by far the best. Several nights later a local television crew showed up and we were on the eleven o'clock news.

We had to guard the house during the day in shifts. That meant we got excused absences from school. We would sit on the front porch or the roof and watch the cars go by, making sure that no one stopped and toured the house outside of normal business hours.

I don't know how much money we raised from the haunted house, but it was a lot. It helped us to win The Hastings Award that year and wrest it away from Columbia, our arch rival school.

Columbia opened in 1966, two years after Walker. The two schools were located about ten miles apart. Walker had the distinction of being the first school built in DeKalb County with an air conditioning system. Columbia not only had an air conditioning system but an Olympic-size pool as well. All of the DeKalb County school swim teams used the pool for competitions.

Gordon High was the closest school in proximity to Walker. The zoning lines around the end of the county between Walker and Gordon were bizarre, to say the least. As a result, a lot of the students that attended each school were neighbors. The football games between Walker and Gordon were more like organized neighborhood games. Southwest DeKalb High was another neighboring school. A lot of Gresham Park kids moved to the SWD area, so a lot of us knew one another. SWD won the state football championship our senior year.

The faculty at Walker was just as unique as the students. Though we did not realize it at the time, many of the teachers were fresh out of college and not much older than the senior class.

Mr. A was an English and Literature teacher. He taught at Walker for thirty years, from 1969 until 1999. He understood teenagers, as best as one possibly could. His lesson plans consisted of assigning us reading material to which we could relate. We read works such as *The Catcher In The Rye*, *Brighton Rock* and *Lord Of The Flies* while students in other classes were suffering through *Wuthering Heights* and *Beowulf*.

Mr. B was an art teacher and so much more at Walker. He was the Jr. Civitan sponsor, the swim team coach and more a friend than a teacher. Mr. B owned and drove a Formula Vee racecar and was very much into the road racing scene. He introduced a lot of us to the sport and we all began making regular trips to Road Atlanta.

He also oversaw the operation of the Bookroom. I capitalized "Bookroom" because it was one of the most popular meeting places in the school. Located at the intersection of the two main halls, the Bookroom featured a dutch door where those of us lucky enough to work there could lean on, socialize and observe. There was a ping pong table inside, a stereophonic record player and a big "Welcome Race Fans" banner that a member of the Bookroom crew had borrowed from Road Atlanta. Working in the Bookroom was a dream job. At the first of the year we distributed the books. At the end of the year we collected the books and returned them to the shelves. During the school year we swapped out a book that had been damaged or was worn out, distributed books to a new student or collected them from a student that was leaving. In the downtime we played ping pong, read magazines, listened to music on the stereophonic record player or caught up on homework.

The first time I ever saw a National Lampoon magazine was in the Bookroom. It belonged to someone else on the crew and featured an article teaching one how to curse in seven different languages. To go along with the article, the magazine also contained one of those thin vinyl 45 rpm records that were similar to an old floppy disk. Moon and I put the record on the stereophonic player, followed along in the magazine and had a foreign language lesson that was definitely not a part of the mainstream curriculum.

You never saw the principal at Walker very much. He was busy with administration, although we did hear from him quite a bit when he would do the morning announcements. In the days before email and the internet, school news and communication was broadcast over a speaker box located in each classroom. If something was pertinent, you wrote it down.

As students, the ones we came in contact with the most were the assistant principals. Mr. O was in charge of discipline, which was much simpler back then. If you were a boy and were sent to Mr. O's office, it generally meant one of three things was going to happen. Three days detention, three days suspension or three licks. To me, the choice was always pretty clear. Three days after school? Yeah, I'm really going to pick that one. Three days suspension and no credit for three days worth of classwork? I don't think so. Give me three swats and let's forget about it. Years after Walker, a friend and I went to a Braves game at the old Atlanta Stadium and were sitting in the club level seats. A man and his two sons came in and sat down next to us. It was Mr. O. I jumped up, shook his hand and told him that I had graduated from Walker in '73." He smiled and said, "I'm sorry, but I really don't remember you." "Well," I told him, "I guess if you don't remember me, that's a good thing!" We had a good laugh, sat down and watched the Braves lose another one.

Mr. J was the assistant principal in charge of attendance. If you got caught skipping school or were a confirmed truant, Mr. J was the one that dealt with you. He was a good man and became principal at Stone Mountain High.

Then there was the coaching staff. First and foremost was Coach. Everyone at Walker and beyond knew him. Coach was funny, witty and had a distinct personality. He was an assistant football coach, became head coach my junior and senior seasons and also coached the boys' and the girls' tennis teams. He attended all of the reunions years later and his mind was still as sharp as a tack. Several of us sat and talked with him at our forty year reunion. He could remember specific football games, plays, series of plays, how much time was on the clock and on which down a certain play occurred.

Coach Jay was the first coach I came in contact with at Walker. He was the man who taught me how to play football. He was my coach for three years, starting in the eighth grade and for two more seasons when he moved up to B-team coach.

Coach H was an assistant coach on the football team as well as the head baseball coach during my junior and senior years. One day in drafting class, a friend and I decided that we wanted to go to The Varsity for lunch. The drafting teacher had a rule concerning venturing forth as such. You either got no credit for that day's class or three licks and if you got caught, "I don't know you." We took our three swats, climbed into my friend's Mustang and headed toward North Avenue. When we got back, Coach H was waiting for us at the top of the hill by the parking lot. He took us back to class. "Uh, huh, you got caught, didn't you?" the drafting teacher laughed. Coach H said to me, "See me before practice today." My heart sank. Three licks from a teacher was one thing, but three from a football coach would light you up like a pinball machine. There was generally nothing between your glutes and the wood but a pair of jockey shorts.

After school I made my way to the locker room, took a deep breath, opened the coaches' office door and went to Coach H's desk. He looked at me and said, "You owe me ten extra wind sprints after practice today. And tomorrow bring me a bag of Beechnut." I walked out of the room on air. Ten extra wind sprints, a bag of chewing tobacco and I was off the hook. Ten extra wind sprints were never easier to run.

That evening I drove to the store and bought a bag of Beechnut. A sixteen year old could do things like that back then. Then something on the shelf caught my eye. "Let me have a plug of Brown's Mule, too," I said. I didn't know anything about chewing tobacco, but it was in a plastic wrapper and had a picture of a red mule on it. I figured it was the least I could do since he had let me off relatively easy. The next morning I went into the coaches' office, put the bag of Beechnut and the plug of Brown's Mule on Coach H's desk before heading up to homeroom. At practice that afternoon I asked him, "Hey, Coach, did you get the Brown's Mule?" "Yeah," he said, "and it tasted like Brown's Mule."

I would be remiss if I wrote a chapter about Walker High School and did not mention Mrs. P. She was a substitute teacher and was a fixture, so much so that her picture was in the yearbook with the faculty. A substitute teacher generally meant a day off from class. Not so with her. She was a large woman, did not take any

85

monkeyshines off of anybody and did not suffer fools gladly. She thought nothing about pulling a student out of class and hauling that student to the office. I ran afoul of her once and only once, in the eighth grade. She dragged me out of class by the ear but didn't take me to the office. Instead she backed me up against the wall, stuck her finger in my face and said, "Listen here. I can be your best friend or your worst enemy. The choice is yours." I went back into the classroom, sat down, kept my mouth shut and did my work.

I cannot think of a better place and a time to go to high school than when we were at Walker. I loved it and cherish the memories more each day. I was never a star student by any stretch of the imagination. But as a dear friend put it, "We were involved." And she was right. The involvement, the student life, the faculty, the sports, the friendships and everything about it were what made it so great. Walker is a different school now with a different name. Millions of dollars have been poured into the building. It is huge and imposing. But Walker is not and never will be gone. As long as there is one of us left, she will forever be in our hearts and in our minds. We are The Warhawks. We are Crimson. We are Silver. We always have been. We always will be.

Moon

Moon was the closest thing that I ever had to a brother. He and I met in the Cub Scouts at the age of nine years old. We went to different schools as kids and lived in different areas of Gresham Park, but we knew each other nonetheless. We played on the same baseball team when we were ten years old. We saw each other at the ballpark and around town. It wasn't until high school that we became friends. We had the same English class together in the tenth grade. That was where we really hit it off and became best friends.

He was called Moon because he had a large, round face and when he smiled or grinned he looked just like the man in the moon. Moon was a big guy. He stood over six feet at fifteen years old and had long arms and legs. He was as strong as a bull and a ferocious football player. Unfortunately, that was the only sport he was proficient in. When we were kids playing baseball, he was afraid of the ball. The pitcher would start his windup and Moon would start backing out of the batter's box. We once spent a whole practice with the coaches trying to teach him to stay in the box. They put bats on the ground behind his heels, but it didn't do any good. He would back out every time. He wasn't very good with a glove either and usually played right field. Playing basketball with him was just as painful. Literally. In the pickup games at the gym as guys came down the court, he would forearm them across the nose just like in football. It almost caused an altercation more than once. I would try to explain to him that you couldn't throw forearms in basketball, but that was all he knew how to do. It got even uglier when he tried to shoot the ball. He never learned that in order to make the ball go in the basket you had to shoot it on an arc and make it spin using a little bit of touch. Moon would get the ball, turn and fire it at the backboard like a rocket. It would ricochet off, often almost taking someone's head with it in the process. If it wasn't a game where he could knock you on your butt, he was lost.

In football, he was the point man on the kickoff return team. What that meant was that he was in the middle of the front line. At the kickoff, as the rest of the team fell back into coverage, Moon would give a rebel yell and charge the kicker. The kicker would usually be watching the flight of the ball. Moon would hit him high and hard, taking him out of the play and sometimes the game. Once was all it took. After that, the kicker would usually fall on the ground or find some other means of getting out of the way. In a game against Columbia, their kicker turned and ran as fast as he could in the opposite direction.

Moon was a good natured fellow and made friends easily. He could talk to anyone. The problem was that he had the propensity to stretch the truth a little and sometimes quite a bit. I learned over time to know when he was telling a whopper. I would just let him talk, nod my head and roll up my pants legs, because it was getting deep.

He could be caring and compassionate and ornery and bullying. I think one of the reasons that we got along so well was that I would not let him push me around. When he started to try I would stand up to him and give it right back. I wouldn't put up with it and he knew it. We actually got into a fight once in our early twenties. I can't remember what it was about, no doubt over some silly reason lost in the fog of the past. All I remember is that it was not pretty. It was at his house. It started in the den in front of the fireplace and wound up down the hill at the bottom of the driveway. It ended when we looked at each other, burst out crying, hugged each other's neck and swore that it would never happen again, which it did not. I woke up the next morning with two black eyes. He didn't have a mark on him. Upon seeing me, my parents demanded to know what had happened. I told them that Moon and I got into a fight. They didn't believe me. They were convinced I was trying to cover something up. They asked Moon about it and when he told them that that was indeed what had happened, they didn't believe him either. My father wouldn't talk to me for a week, which was a pretty common thing at that point in time.

There has never been anyone in the world that could make me laugh like Moon. The adventures that we had, the trouble that we got into and the stories that we lived are countless. When I say the trouble that we got into, it was usually the trouble that I got into. Moon would come up with some brilliant idea and I was all too willing to carry it out. It always landed me in hot water, either with my parents, teachers or the local law enforcement agencies. He always managed to escape unscathed while I took the brunt of the punishment.

The first time we went to the races at Road Atlanta was during our junior year in high school. We went in my father's old brown Chevy Apache pickup and took a tent, two sleeping bags, a pack of bologna, a loaf of bread, a jar of mayo and a case of Schlitz. For two sixteen year old boys, this was the ultimate. After that initial trip, we recruited friends and before long there were ten to fifteen of us headed to the track. We learned to camp more civilized. We brought campers, large family tents, tables, chairs and even girls. We once even rented a Winnebago. One night as we stood around the campfire, I looked at Moon and said, "It's come a long way from baloney, bread and Schlitz, hasn't it?" He laughed and said, "Yeah, it has. We know a good time when we see one."

With nothing particular to do one Saturday morning, we were riding around in Moon's new Z28 Camaro and wound up somewhere in Decatur. We stopped at a red light and turned right onto Glenwood Road. As we turned, there was a young black man about our age walking up the opposite sidewalk wearing absolutely nothing but a pair of sneakers. Words would not come out of my mouth. All I could do was point at him. We rode in silence for a second, then Moon looked at me and said, "I've gotta see 'em lock him up, man!" I turned around and looked and he was crossing the street, heading into a small grocery store. Moon whipped the Camaro around and by this time the young man was bopping back across the crosswalk carrying in one hand a paper sack with a loaf of bread sticking out of it. He headed back down the sidewalk, seemingly in complete control of his faculties. There were people standing at the end of driveways and streets watching him. A car in front of us stopped and he leaned in the window, chatted with them for a second and pointed back up the street. Then he continued on down the sidewalk and turned up one of the side streets, apparently heading home to make himself a sandwich. Hopefully it wasn't a BLT. Moon and I looked at each other and howled with laughter. "Man, nobody is gonna believe what we just saw!" he yelled. It was one of the funniest and most bizarre things that I have ever seen in my entire life.

Moon was the best man at my wedding. He and my wife Mary Jane became very close. Mary Jane was British. Moon and I had always shared a kindred connection

with the Old Country. The night before the wedding
he told me, "Man, I can't believe you're marrying an
Englishwoman!" The three of us did a lot of things
together. One spring morning in the early Eighties,
we went to Applebee's for champagne brunch. We left
there, bought a case of beer and headed toward Arabia
Mountain in my pickup truck. Along the way, Mary
Jane shook up a beer, looked at Moon and sprayed it in is
face. It was on then. He sprayed her back and they both
sprayed me. I attempted to spray them and steer at the
same time. The entire cab was soaking wet and we were
laughing hysterically. We climbed Arabia Mountain,
sat on a boulder and spent the entire afternoon talking
and gazing at the Atlanta skyline in the distance. Years
later, Mary Jane told me Moon had once told her that if
anything ever happened to me, he would take care of her.

Moon and I were both lifelong Georgia Bulldog fans
and in our mid twenties we began to go to the games.
Like Road Atlanta, the Saturday afternoons in Athens
had humble beginnings. We went to see the Bulldogs
play the Temple Owls on Halloween during Herschel's
sophomore season. Moon's brother was in his senior
year at UGA and had tickets for us. We stopped by
his apartment Saturday morning to pick up the tickets.
The keg parties were already in full swing on all of the
balconies in the complex. I looked at Moon and said,
"You know, it's a good thing we didn't come over here
right out of high school." "Oh, God," he replied, "we'd

have never made it to basketball season."

Once again we recruited friends and within a few years there were ten to fifteen of us in our tailgate camp. We set up on the lawn at the arts building on Jackson Street and did the whole nine yards with food, beverages and portable accommodations. Moon was a regular guy and every football Saturday at nine in the morning he would head down to the men's room for his morning constitution. One Saturday he stuck the sports section under his arm, bopped down the hill and attempted to open the door to the arts building. The door was locked. After rattling the handle and banging on the door, he searched out and found a campus police officer. Moon colorfully explained the situation to him. The officer opened the door and Moon went in, sat down and happily checked the point spreads for the day's games.

My father passed away in the pre-dawn hours on a Wednesday in early October. When I returned home from the hospital, the first person I called was Moon. I lost it when I heard his voice on the other end of the line. "He's gone, Moon," I sobbed. "He's gone." "I'm on my way down now," said Moon. I lived south of Atlanta, in Henry County and he lived north, in Canton. I used to kid him that he was going to keep moving north until he wound up in Tennessee and wearing orange overalls. Two hours later he pulled into my driveway. By then I was an inconsolable basket case, but seeing my friend immediately made me feel better. He stayed with me for two days. He called work and told them that he would not be in for the remainder of the week. We sat on the back deck and reminisced about the old times. We had a few drinks and enjoyed the beautiful early fall weather. We laughed and I cried. Each time the emotions would rise up he would comfort me until they ebbed. I do not know what I would have done without him there with me. The two of us rode to the funeral together. He sat on the front row next to me. We rode back to my mother's house together for the traditional post service gathering. He took me home and made sure that I was okay. After he left, I walked outside to the deck. I thought about how long we had been friends and how lucky I was to have him in my life. While tailgaiting at one of the Georgia games a few weeks later, I told him how much it meant that he had stayed with me when my father died. He looked at me and said, "Hey, that's what friends do." We gave each other a big bro hug. I never felt closer to any man in my life.

Four years later, on a Saturday morning in early April, the phone rang. It was Moon's stepson. "This is a pretty tough thing for me to have to tell you," he said, "but Moon got killed in a car wreck last night." The words did not sound real. All that would come out of my mouth was "Oh, my God, Oh, my God." Mary Jane came running out shouting, "What's the matter? What's the matter?" She told me later that my face was literally shaking. I looked at her and cried, "Moon got killed in a car wreck last night." "Moon?" she cried. "Moon? Oh, God, no, not Moon!" She sat down on the deck bench and burst into tears. I sat down next to her and we held each other for what seemed like an eternity, both sobbing uncontrollably.

Moon always envisioned himself behind the wheel of a racecar at Road Atlanta. The only problem was that he couldn't drive. He never grasped the concept of going fast without going fast. The curves were the scariest. He didn't understand slowing as you approached the curve, tapping the brake pedal and then accelerating halfway through. Instead he would run into the curve at full speed and slam on the brakes. When I heard the details of the wreck, I knew exactly what had happened. His neighbor had just bought a Porsche 944. He and Moon took it out for a ride. Moon convinced his neighbor to let him drive and he failed to negotiate a curve. The car flipped and landed on the driver's side of the top. Moon was killed instantly. His neighbor walked away from the wreck with minor injuries. I was told later that it was estimated that he was going 105 mph when he went into the curve.

Later that year, the phone rang on the night before the Georgia-Auburn game. It was Moon's wife. He had been cremated and she told us that she had spread his ashes on the field at Sanford Stadium that morning.

She had contacted the athletic office earlier that week and told them that her husband had passed away. She explained that although he was not an alumnus he had been a lifelong Bulldog, was a season ticket holder and a supporter of the Alumni Association. She said that she wanted to put his ashes on the field. She also said that she was going to do so no matter what they told her, even if she had to climb fences in the middle of the night. They told her that they would get back with her. She received a call and was told to be at gate such and such at such and such a time the following morning. A security guard let her in the gate and she walked the length of the field, spreading Moon's ashes from end zone to end zone.

I don't believe in ghosts, but I have seen two in my life. One of those occasions happened the next day. At one point, Auburn's quarterback rolled out to the left. There was no one around him. All of a sudden his upper body went back, his feet tangled up, he spun around and went down hard. Larry Munson, The Legendary Voice Of The Bulldogs, growled over the radio, "I don't know what happened there." I knew exactly what had happened. Moon had hit the quarterback, slung him around and to the turf. Then I saw him rise up on one knee, dressed in the Red and Black and wearing the Silver Britches. He pointed his right index finger into the clear autumn sky and gave his signature rebel yell. He was there, Between the Hedges forever.

The Duke

Duke and I went to kindergarten together. We attended different elementary schools and played Little League ball against each other. I got to know him in eighth grade gym class.

Gym class for eighth graders was first or sixth period. In other words, it was the first class of the day or the last. We had it first period, which meant you left homeroom, hurried down to the locker room, changed into your gym clothes and went to the designated spot for roll call. All this occurred within the space of about ten minutes. At the end of class you would go back to the locker room, change back into your school clothes, lock up your gym clothes in your basket or put them in your gym bag to take home to be washed, go back upstairs to your school locker, grab your books and head to class while negotiating the traffic in the hall. All of this occurred within the space of about ten minutes as well. Come to think of it, it's really not that much different than a morning commute to work as an adult.

Duke and I became friends during our first spring football practice. Our lockers were next to each other. Spring practice was in March. It lasted for three weeks and I received a baptism by fire on the very first day. Underclassmen practiced separately for an hour or so and then were brought up to scrimmage against the varsity. We basically were live tackling dummies. They put me out on the left corner and on the very first play ran a sweep right at me. The fullback and the blocking back were leading the ball carrier. I squared up to meet them and the blocking back yelled, "Watch the corner!" The fullback yelled, "I got him," and hit me so hard that my chinstrap and one shoe came off. I flew airborne backwards and was, I swear, laughing in mid air. I hit the ground on my butt and skidded along before coming to a stop. I found my shoe, sat down and put it back on. On his way back to the huddle the fullback grabbed my arm and pulled me up just as I finished tying my shoe. He said, "All right, little man, good hit, good hit!" I was sure he was talking about the hit he put on me, but he slapped the top of my helmet and my shoulder pads. I found my chinstrap, buckled it back up and took my place at left corner, ready to go again. It was the hardest that I was ever hit, before or since.

Spring training culminated in an intrasquad game at Panthersville Stadium. The game was called the Crimson and Silver game and the way the teams were divided was simple. The Crimson team was the first string linemen and the second string backs, the Silver was the second string linemen and the first string backs. We suited up in full game uniforms and rode the bus to the stadium. The game was officiated by GHSA officials. It was played at night under the lights. It was, for all intents and purposes, a real game. The players and the coaches certainly approached it as such. The idea was to give the veteran players a game at the end of three grueling weeks of practice and to see how the younger players performed under game conditions. I didn't play in the game that year because I was a rising freshman who would play on the B-team the next season. Duke played in it because halfway through spring practice he was promoted to the varsity. He played halfback and switched to quarterback during our sophomore season. He became a starter our junior year.

Duke was the best athlete that I had or have ever seen. He had that blessed ability to excel in any sport that he played. I really don't know where the name "Duke" came from. It was hung on him sometime during elementary school. I always called him Duke because he was the best player on the field. By our senior year he played quarterback on offense, safety on defense, did all of the punting and all of the kick returns. He was the Region 7-AAA Player Of The Year, despite playing on a team that won only one game.

Besides his prowess in football he was an excellent baseball player as well. He played centerfield, first base, pitcher and catcher. He had a cannon for an arm and could throw a ball further and harder than anybody I had ever seen in my life. In gym class we played basketball, volleyball and dodgeball. Duke excelled in all of them.

He had Major League Baseball scouts looking at him

by our junior year. Baseball games were played at the
school fields back then. One spring afternoon Walker
was playing at home and Moon and I went to see the
game. Duke was playing centerfield. At one point
there was a runner on second and the ball was hit high
and deep into center. There was no fence on the field
at Walker, just a hill that led up to the tennis courts and
the gym parking lot. Duke caught the ball at the base of
the hill. Under normal circumstances the runner could
have tagged up, rounded third and scored easily. It was
not normal circumstances that day. Duke pushed off of
the bottom of the hill and let go of a cannon shot toward
third base. The ball bounced once in front of the third
baseman who caught the ball and the runner slid into
the tag. The umpire simply raised his right fist with his
elbow bent. You're out. It was a three hundred foot
throw, one bounce and an easy out on a runner tagging
from second. Moon and I just looked at each other
dumbfounded.

Duke was drafted by the Braves but chose instead to go
to college on a football scholarship. He was a starting
quarterback for four years and after his senior season
he was selected in the eighth round of the NFL draft.
He made the team as a backup quarterback. An injury
sidelined the starting quarterback and suddenly Duke
was the starting quarterback on Monday Night Football.
I'll never forget watching that game as long as I live.

A buddy and I went to another friend's house to watch the game with a group of guys. All the pregame hoopla was going on and the MNF crew was talking about what had happened and who would be starting. Then they cut to a shot of Duke warming up on the sidelines. The last time I had seen him suited up was our final high school game. To see him wearing a pro uniform and warming up before a Monday Night game was mind boggling.

As mind boggling as that may have been, it was nothing compared to what happened next. The first series of downs Duke took the team down the field. At one point he hit the wide receiver with a bullet on an out pattern to the sidelines, prompting Howard Cosell to exclaim in that inimitable voice of his, "I really like this kid from Decatuh Geohgia!" We all looked at each other and laughed. It was unbelievable.

They would lose by one point that night, but Duke finished the season as the starter and the team won two of the last five games. He was the starting quarterback for the next two years. After playing eight seasons he retired, returned home to Georgia and became a successful businessman.

Years later his son played quarterback for a major college team and on into the pros. The first time I saw him play on television it was, as Yogi Berra used to say, "like deja vu, all over again." Early in the game he ran for about a twenty yard gain. He looked just like his dad running, with that loping, rawboned gait. And my mind went back to Panthersville Stadium some thirty years earlier. The memories are there. They always will be.

Quarter Pounders and Ground Pounders

In the mid Sixties, McDonald's opened up on Gresham Road across from the plaza. It wasn't one of the original McDonald's with the arches on the outside of the building, but it was close. There wasn't a dining room. That would be added later. The order and pickup windows were the only things inside the building. There was a walkway out front with round concrete tables and benches. Hamburgers were fifteen cents and a shake was a quarter. It was long before the Big Mac and the Quarter Pounder graced the menu. I refuse to even mention the McRib.

McDonald's quickly became a hangout. Like Clifton Springs, there was always a steady stream of cars around the building and parking lot. The cars that slowly circled the building and eased into the parking spaces would make any classic car collector drool today. Those were times before Ralph Nader, the oil embargo and the catalytic converter. A black 1970 Chevelle SS with white panel stripes would cruise into the lot, followed by a yellow Mach 1 with black panels. An orange '69 Roadrunner would be close behind, along with a gold Z28 Camaro.

The boys wouldn't be the only ones making the scene. A girl would pull in driving a yellow and black Comet GT.

Another would roll in behind the wheel of a silver Dodge Charger with black custom side striping. Besides the souped up coupes there were the custom sedans as well. A red and white Vega with a highly modified 350 cubic inch engine would lope into the lot. A Ford Fairlane with slotted disc wheels and a 289 hi-performance engine would pull in and park next to a Chevy II and a Dodge Polara. The driver would get out, join his two friends leaning against the fender of the Polara and discuss paint jobs, girls and four-barrel carburetors.

The parade was not just limited to American iron. A silver blue Austin Healy 3000 would pull in along with a light green Opel GT. A souped up VW would sputter around the building as an orange Karmann Ghia convertible pulled in behind it. A red MGB would roll in followed by a Chevy Corvair Monza. Even after the Corvair parked, it was unsafe. Remember, they were "unsafe at any speed." All of this occurred pretty much every night, even on school nights.

Cars from other parts of town such as Decatur and Forest Park would cruise in as well. There were never really any fights to speak of, at least not that I can recall. More than likely one of the visitors would challenge one of the locals to a drag race. Everyone would pile into their cars to follow the crowd and watch the two asphalt gladiators engage in a contest of speed.

Several years after McDonald's was built, a Dairy Queen

opened three doors down. Then there were two places to cruise and hang out. On a typical summer day, the ritual was to cruise McDonald's, pull into Dairy Queen, check things out there and then head down to Clifton Springs to cruise the beach.

Somewhere along the way, someone who was not really a reliable source told my father that a certain type of contraband was being offered for purchase in the Dairy Queen parking lot. Hence, I was forbidden to go to the Dairy Queen. My father's description of the alleged transactions was not so eloquent and he would tell anyone and everyone who would listen. One afternoon I was at the DQ in my dune buggy, leaning against the fender and talking to a few of my buddies. My father rode by and saw me. The bright yellow Meyers Manx with the white convertible top was hard to miss. He whipped his truck into the parking lot, screeched to a stop behind us and jumped out. He yelled for me to "get that thing home with my [gluteus maximus] in it right now!" He glared at my friends like they were reprobates from Fourteenth Street and climbed back into his truck. He backed up and waited for me to pull out. To say it was embarrassing is an understatement. He followed me home and when I climbed out of the dune buggy he slammed the door to the truck, poked his finger in my chest and said that he had told me about hanging out in that "blankity blank slop chute" and if he ever saw me there again he was "first gonna whip whoever's [gluteus maximus] I was with and then he was gonna whip mine." I always wondered if he would whip one of our defensive ends' [gluteous maximus], had I been there with them. I still went to the Dairy Queen, but I didn't drive the dune buggy there anymore.

A group of us were sitting at one of the concrete tables at McDonald's one Saturday afternoon. One guy told another that he would give him five dollars if he would climb the ladder at the back of the building, walk to the front of the roof and yell an obscenity. Five bucks was big money in those days. He got up, walked to the back of the building, climbed the ladder, walked to the front of the roof and yelled the obscenity. He then climbed back down the ladder, walked back to our table and sat down. An off duty police officer who worked there as a security guard approached our table. He really didn't work much. He mostly just harassed us youngsters and leaned against the trunk of his car gaining weight. "Exactly what the [Hades] do you think you were doing?" he asked the obscenity yeller.

"Expressing my views."

"On what?"

"Things in general."

"You know I can arrest you."

"For what?"

"Trespassing and vulgar language in a public place."

"There wasn't a "no trespassing" sign back there. Besides, aren't you off duty?"

The officer looked at us and said, "All of y'all need to get out of here right now." We complied. Two days later there was a cage around the ladder with a padlock on it.

Moon and I were cruising around one night and pulled into McDonald's to get something to eat. A buddy of ours worked there and it was nearing closing time. I pulled up to the drive-in window. He came to the window, looked around kind of nervously and said, "Y'all pull over in one of the spaces over there and wait a minute." We did as he said, not really knowing what was going on. A minute later our buddy ran out and stuck a big bag of food through the driver's side window. "Here," he said, "take this and get outta here." I pulled out and Moon started looking through the bag. It was full of Big Macs, Quarter Pounders, fries and apple pies. We both started laughing. I pulled over into the lot at the shopping center across the street and parked at the top. We emptied the bag. "Man," said Moon through a mouthful of hamburger, " I hope he doesn't get fired for this." "Yeah, me too," I said, while shoveling in a handful of fries. "We need to start doing this every night."

The next day at school I asked my buddy exactly how he was able to do such a thing. He explained that at closing time the food that was left over was thrown away. "I take home a bag every night," he said. "It's one of the perks of working there. Just don't make a habit out of showing up every night." I didn't tell him that was exactly what I had suggested we start doing.

One day I was at South DeKalb Mall visiting my cousin who worked there. A Walker girl named Carol stopped by also. Carol was a beautiful girl with long blonde hair. She was a cheerleader and drove a red 1970 Datsun 240Z. For some reason that I cannot begin to remember, I needed a ride home and Carol offered to give me a lift. It was a ride I will never forget. She hit the entrance ramp to I-20 and floored it. It was summertime and the windows were down. She was talking away to me and laughing with that blonde hair flying. I happened to look over at the speedometer and we were running a hundred miles an hour at five in the afternoon on I-20 between Candler Road and Flat Shoals Road. I was sitting there trying to act cool, but those were the days before seat belts. In reality, my butt had grown fingers that were clamped to the bottom of the seat. We made it home in one piece. She let me out of the car and tore off up the hill toward her house. I looked around to see if Brain or Bubba-Bubba had seen me get out of that red 240Z with Carol driving. No such luck. I sat down on the front steps and realized that it had been like being on a thrill ride at Six Flags. It scared the crap out of me, but I loved it! Tearing down the expressway in a red sports car with a beautiful girl at the wheel? That's the stuff dreams and songs are made of. The memories are there. They always will be.

Petroleum Transfer

I got my first real job when I was sixteen years old. The summer before my junior year of high school a Field Distributor for The American Oil Company hired me as a Petroleum Transfer Engineer. In other words, I pumped gas. The girl I was dating was a Quick Nourishment Point Of Purchase Sales Associate. She worked at McDonald's.

School had been out for about a week when Moon gave me a call. His father traded at the American station and had helped him get a job for the summer. They needed someone to work the evening shift during the week and all day Saturday. I applied, was hired and started the following day.

The owner's name was Mr. Burly. He was gruff with us teenagers, but under the surface he was a very kind and generous man. Moon and I were thrilled to have jobs. We made a dollar and a half an hour and my first paycheck was a little over sixty dollars. I thought I was rich. I spent most of my money that summer on gas, eight track tapes, hamburgers, milk shakes and movies. I did manage to save a little and at the end of the summer I was able to go to South DeKalb Mall and buy all of my school clothes on my own.

Gas was twenty eight cents for regular, thirty three cents for midgrade and a whopping forty two cents a gallon for premium. I remember looking at the price of the premium and wondering how gasoline could be such an astronomical price. I could fill up my dune buggy with regular for a little less than three dollars. One day on a whim I filled up with premium and it cost me over four bucks. I was racked with guilt for a week at the thought of spending four dollars for a tank of gas, especially when I could have bought two eight track tapes instead.

Mr. Burly's son in law was the mechanic at the station. His name was Junior. He was very skinny but walked like an ape and sang *Me And You And A Dog Named Boo* all summer. He called Moon and I both "Sport." I'm not sure if he even knew our names.

Mr. Lyons was part owner of the station and insisted that we call him "Lyons." Not "Mr. Lyons" or his first name "Harry." Just Lyons. Lyons drove a beat up old Ford Falcon. The back seat and most of the front seat was filled with junk from the service station. I never saw him take any of it out or put anything in. I guess he just rode around with the same junk in it all the time.

Lyons had served on Iwo Jima but you never would have known it. He moved and talked very slow and had the worst case of irritable bowel syndrome ever known to man. Once or twice a week without fail the phone would ring about eight thirty in the morning. "Gresham Park American, can I help you?" I would answer. "Hey, this is Lyons," the voice on the other end of the line would drawl. "I got the G.I.'s again this mornin'. Tell Burly I'll try to be in this afternoon." He never would come in. And when he did, he didn't do anything. He never worked on cars, never answered the phone, never stocked the shelves and he certainly never pumped gas. He mostly just sat around and talked with the old men who showed up every day and hung around the gas station.

One of the things that made working at the station so interesting was the people you would meet. One guy drove a pale yellow station wagon, had a brown moustache, never smiled and always smelled like coffee. He would come in once a week and fill up. It did not matter if it had been raining for two days straight, he would always tell you that he had just spent two and a half hours washing and waxing his automobile and he did not want one drop of gas spilled on it. He carried a little spiral notebook in his back pocket and was always writing down notes as you worked, presumably concerning your service or lack thereof. The gas cap was on the side of the station wagon and the first time I met him I made the mistake of placing the cap on the top of the car. This was after the two and a half hours washing and waxing spiel. He snatched the cap off of the top of the car, slammed it on top of the pump, muttered under his breath and wrote something in his notebook. I picked up the windshield cleaning fluid and started to pull a couple of paper towels out of the dispenser. He looked at me and said, "Don't put any of that blankity-blank blank on my windshield. I just spent two and a half hours washing and waxing this automobile." He then stood with his head literally over my left shoulder as I pumped the gas. A tiny drop spilled on the fender as I removed the nozzle and before I could wipe it off he cursed a blasphemous obscenity, pulled a handkerchief out of his pocket and wiped the dribble off of the fender. Then he wrote something in his notebook, refused to pay me and walked inside the station. Mr. Burly asked how he was doing and he stated that he was doing fine but he didn't think too much of the help, meaning me. He told Mr. Burly that he had just spent two and a half hours washing and waxing his automobile and I spilled gas all over the fender and scratched his top with the gas cap. He paid him for the tank of gas, demanded a receipt, suggested that I be fired and left in a huff. I must have looked either sheepish or shocked because Mr. Burly put his hand on my shoulder and laughed. "Don't worry, Sport, I'm not going to fire you," he said. "He treats everybody that way. Junior changed his oil once. He stood over Junior's shoulder and then told me I needed to fire Junior 'cause he spilled a little bit of oil on the valve cover. Another time we were doin' some work on his car and Lyons gave him a ride back home. Lyons ran through a yellow light and before he got back to the station he had called and told me I oughta fire Lyons for endangerin' the life of a customer with his reckless drivin'. He's an [embellished gluteus maximus]." I wasn't going to argue the point.

That summer was one of those that about four o'clock every day the bottom would fall out. At the height of the deluge some little old lady would inevitably pull into the far island at the top of the lot. I would put on my poncho and walk to the car. She would roll her window down a half an inch and say, "Could you tell me how to get to I-20?" The station was located on a main road right off of I-20. "You pull out and take a left. The ramp to I-20 west is right there," I would say with all of the politeness I could muster during a driving rainstorm while pointing at the Interstate sign. "Cross the bridge and the eastbound entrance is on the left." "Oh, so it is! I missed the sign. Thank you, young man," she would say and pull slowly out of the station while I slogged back inside. This would happen at least twice a day and was not limited to little old ladies. It crossed both gender lines and included all age groups.

It was the dawn of the Seventies, so we saw all kinds of makes and models of cars. The first Pontiac Trans-Am I ever saw was at the gas station. It was white with blue panel stripes and had a 455 cubic inch engine with a shaker hood scoop. I had never seen anything like it in my life. As I filled it up, the owner told me that it was a new package for the Firebird and that they also were available painted blue with white panels. He must have seen me drooling, because he asked if I would like to check the oil. I couldn't get the hood up fast enough. I gawked and marveled for a few minutes and then he asked me, "Aren't you going to check the oil?" I had completely forgotten The Routine of Proper Service. I pulled out the dipstick, wiped it clean, re-inserted it and pulled it out again. The oil was a clean, rich gold color and right at the full marker. "Looks great," I said. "I knew that it would," he said, grinning at me as I closed the hood.

The Routine of Proper Service was as follows. You would greet the customer courteously and ask how you could be of service. You would pull the nozzle, set the pump and start it running with the flow locked at the slowest speed, wipe the windshield and ask the customer if they would like the oil checked. You would then check the pump and stop it if necessary. Finally you would check the air in the tires and top them up, take the customer's money and get them change if necessary. It was a procedure that became more efficient with repetition and eventually like clockwork. That procedure went out the window one day when a gentleman pulled in driving a '57 Chevy sedan. He told me how much gas he needed and I went to the back of the car. Most gas caps were located behind the tag back then, so I bent down and tried to pull the tag forward. The tag wouldn't budge. I looked on each side of the big finned fenders. No gas cap. I looked under the car to no avail and finally had to do the unthinkable. I walked up to the window and asked the driver, "I'm sorry to ask, but where is the gas cap?" He laughed, got out of the car, walked to the back and flipped open a door on the chrome trim above the driver's side taillight. There was the gas cap. "Believe me, you're not the first one to ask," he said. "It's the same on a '55 and '56, only the entire assembly folds down." I thanked him and made a mental note. Sure enough, a couple of days later a souped up '55 pulled in. I folded down the taillight, started the pump going and went about The Routine of Proper Service.

A blonde girl would pull into the station from time to time in a light green Plymouth Roadrunner. She never bought gas. She would just smile, bat her eyes and say, "Would you mind cleaning my windshield?" In my youthful bliss and naiveté I did not realize that she knew exactly what she was doing. She was always wearing a pair of cut off jeans that were way above the line. As you cleaned the driver's side, she would move her legs about into various positions and poses. Staring and wiping the windshield beyond clean, I would occasionally look up and make eye contact. She would smile and bat her eyes again. I would then replace the windshield wipers and she would say, "Thanks, honey. Bye, now." She would drive away, leaving me staring at the rear of her car while holding a paper towel and a bottle of cleaning solution.

Two a day football practices started in mid-August and Mr. Burly let Moon and I work in the afternoons between practices and in the evenings afterward. When school started I worked a few Saturdays but between school and football it was a little too much. I told Mr. Burly and offered to continue until he found someone else. He told me that was fine and that he already had someone lined up. He wished me good luck in football. I learned a lot that summer as a Petroleum Transfer Engineer, lessons that I would have never learned in books and some that I have never forgotten. The memories are there. They always will be.

The Grove

Gresham Park really didn't have a rival neighborhood. The closest to a rival would have been Cedar Grove. Cedar Grove is a community about five miles south of Gresham Park down Bouldercrest Road. Cedar Grove is not as big as Gresham Park and was more rural in the time that we boomers were growing up.

The reason that there really wasn't much of a rivalry probably stemmed from the fact that we all went to school together. The elementary schools were separate, but Walker was the high school that Gresham Park and Cedar Grove were districted to. You were either a Grove Boy or a Grove Girl or a Gresham Park Boy or a Gresham Park Girl. East Atlanta was close to Gresham Park as well but the majority of kids from there went to either East Atlanta High or Roosevelt, which were both City of Atlanta schools.

Cedar Grove High School did not open until the fall of 1972 and by then a lot of Gresham Park families were beginning to leave. One of the reasons that Cedar Grove High was built was to ease the overcrowding at Walker. There wasn't much of a sports rivalry between the two schools because they were in different classifications and regions. The two schools did not play against each other in athletic competitions until 1974. Cedar Grove's first graduating class was in 1975.

In games played outside of the jurisdiction of the GHSA, the rivalry was much more competitive. The last year I played organized baseball was when I was thirteen years old. We won our league in Gresham Park and advanced to the playoffs. We traveled to Cedar Grove to play the champion of the Bouldercrest league. It was a best of three series. They beat us handily the first two games. It was the end of the season for us and the end of baseball for me. In non-organized sports things got a lot more heated. The Grove Boys backyard football team took on any and all comers and even traveled to different neighborhoods to play. They were fearsome and definitely did not play two hand touch below the waist.

As I grew into my early twenties I began to hang out quite a bit in Cedar Grove. I became friends with two brothers who lived in the heart of the Grove on Bouldercrest Road. I spent so much time at their house and in the surrounding vicinity that I became somewhat of an Honorary Grove Boy.

By the late Seventies Cedar Grove, like so many other communities, had changed and many of her lifelong residents had moved away. Some were never heard from again. Others remained in touch for a while before drifting away. Still others are friends even to this day. I remained close friends with the two brothers even after their family left The Grove. We eventually grew up and started families of our own. We talked often and saw one another occasionally, when time and logistics would permit.

The two brothers are gone now and much too soon. Others are gone as well. But they are all alive and well in the hearts and souls of those of us who loved them. Some bonds are never broken, even in death. The memories are there. They always will be.

The Flight

As early as 1969 not only Gresham Park and Atlanta, but also the entire country had begun to change. Families began to move from the communities in close proximity to the cities to those further out and beyond. The migration began as a trickle in Gresham Park. Within the space of a couple of years, the move began en masse.

Many moved within close proximity. Moon's family moved to Cedar Grove, which would undergo a similar transition in the late Seventies through the mid Eighties. Others moved to the Southwest DeKalb area and many to Rockdale County and Conyers. Still others moved to other parts of the state and the country. Within five years the demographics of Gresham Park had completely changed.

My parents and I left Gresham Park in 1973. We lived in Spanish Trace Apartments for the summer while our new house was being built. For an eighteen year old boy, living in Spanish Trace was like living in heaven. It was a predominately singles' apartment complex with a clubhouse, tennis courts and three swimming pools, which were lined and filled with bikini clad beauties in their early to mid twenties. Our apartment was right next to one of those pools and my friends and I spent a great portion of the summer there. Right after graduation I landed a summer job at the complex working on the maintenance crew. I managed to help two of my friends get jobs there as well and we spent the summer cutting grass, pruning hedges, changing air conditioner filters and hanging out at the pool. I walked to work every morning. My girlfriend lived about a half mile away. I walked to her house in the evenings. Girls came by to see us and to go swimming. There were keg parties at the clubhouse and barbecues by the pool. Life couldn't have been better.

In September it all came crashing down. Our new house was finished and we moved from Spanish Trace to Rex, in northeast Clayton County. I felt like I had moved to Hooterville. Our subdivision was built in the middle of pastureland. There were no trees, no friends and no nubile young ladies hanging around the pool. There was a swimming hole up by the Old Rex Mill. We used to go there, climb the trees and jump into the water, but it wasn't the same as keg parties, barbecues and bikinis.

When our phone was first hooked up we had a party line. I would be talking on the phone and two little old ladies would break into the conversation discussing what hat Flora had worn to church the previous Sunday. My friends who still lived in civilization would fall out laughing. They would want to know if I had to climb the pole and ask Sarah to get me the Douglases up to Cedar Grove.

The one thing that was there that I really liked was an

old country store that was on the main highway. It was a real country store with a wood burning stove in the middle and a checkerboard next to it. I stopped there for gas all the time. They sold homemade cakes and pies, feed and tack, overalls and live bait. It was also the last place I ever saw one of the old Coke machines that you would put a quarter in, open up the top, slide the bottle through the rails, around the corners and then pull it up at the gate that the quarter had unlocked. Progress came to Hooterville a couple of years after we moved there. They tore the old store down and built a drive-in gas station with pumps, a car wash and a kiosk.

I still spent a lot of time in Gresham Park, hanging around with my friends whose families had remained. And I began to resent my parents for moving out of the only place that I had ever known to a barren wasteland fifteen miles south. I wanted to move back to Gresham Park. A couple of buddies and I talked about renting a house there but we never did. It would be several years before we struck out on our own and by that time the lure of the singles' apartments on Memorial Drive between the Perimeter and Stone Mountain was too great to resist. Gresham Park as we knew it was gone forever. Gone, but not forgotten. The memories are there. They always will be.

Friends And Neighbors

I once read a quote that stated, "Each meeting occurs at the precise moment for which it was meant. Usually when it will have the greatest impact on our lives." I grew up surrounded by friends and neighbors who had a profound influence not only on my life but on the lives of others as well.

Jake lived next door to us to our left, going back up the hill toward Boulderview Drive. He was four years older than me and played baseball, football and basketball. I thought he was Superman. He had a little sister who was a wonderful child with a personality as big as she was small. Jake gave me my first dog, a Brittany Spaniel. He was meant to be a hunting dog but was gun shy. He hung around our house and Jake eventually gave him to me. Jake's father owned a flooring company and my father went to work for him managing the warehouse. I worked there for two summers, when I was thirteen and fourteen, unloading trucks of tile to get in shape for football. I wasn't on the payroll and wasn't really an employee, but every week Jake's dad would slip me a twenty and tell me to keep up the good work.

Billy was my best friend in our neighborhood, but Herb was my best friend from another Gresham Park neighborhood. We played on the same baseball team at the ballpark. Like every other kid growing up in the Sixties, our favorite team was the Yankees and our favorite players were Roger Maris and Mickey Mantle. Herb wore Mantle's number seven and I wore Maris's number nine. He was a pitcher and I played first base. We won the AAA Championship in '65. To a bunch of ten year old kids, it was like winning the World Series.

Herb and I were in the Boy Scouts together. We went to the Madison, saw Elvis movies and read Superman comic books. His parents and my parents were best friends. I would ride my bike to Herb's house in the summer and a bunch of us from the neighborhood would camp out in his tree house. He had a big back yard and that was where we played football and baseball. We spent Thanksgivings and Christmases together. We played football together on the B-Team. He was the quarterback and I was the center. We only lost one game that season. It was the best team that I ever played on.

When I was twelve years old I met Beera, who lived on Gresham Road. Beera eventually became one of my best friends. He was called that because a co-worker who couldn't talk plain pronounced his name "Beera."

I met a girl at Walker named Stephanie when I was in the eleventh grade and she was in the ninth. I would run into her after sixth period at school. She would be coming up the stairs from gym class and I would be going down to get ready for football practice. We became fast friends and I began hanging out at her house a lot. Her parents' names were T.L. and Lois. Their family became like my second family.

Their house was one of those to which all of the neighborhood kids naturally gravitated. I have never in my life known two more gracious, kind, unselfish and patient folks in my life than T.L and Lois. They never treated me, or any of us for that matter, as anything other than an equal and a friend. T.L. was a career soldier who worked in the motor pool at The National Guard Armory and supplemented his income by working on VWs. When I first met the family, he worked on them in the driveway and beside the house. When they moved to a larger home on the outskirts of Cedar Grove, he worked out in the carport. After retiring from the Guard, he rented a garage on Fairview Road about two miles from their house and worked there for ten or fifteen years. I painted the sign for the shop when he opened it. The slogan on the sign was "We Get The Bugs Out."

T.L. had a very acerbic sense of humor. Everyone had a nickname. Moon, all six foot two and two hundred twenty pounds of him, was "Tiny." One of the Gresham Park kids, a longhair of whom T.L. was not particularly fond, was "Alice." My father was "Julie." That's all T.L. ever called him. The two of them became very close friends. Daddy would go over and hang around T.L.'s garage at least three or four times a week. I stopped by one winter afternoon and T.L. told me that

Mary Jane "came a-wheelin' in here the other day with the top down, wearin' an overcoat, gloves and a big ol' floppy hat, tellin' me her car was a-makin' a funny noise. I said, "Hell, Mary Jane, it's a Volkswagen. It's supposed to make funny noises!" She left in a huff. I went home, drove the car around the block and didn't hear anything other than the usual Volkswagen funny noises.

When I was drifting in and out of jobs in my late teens and early twenties, T.L. was always good enough to pay me a few bucks to help him out around the garage whenever he could. He taught me a lot about VWs, but the most important lesson he taught me was that I was in no way cut out to be a professional mechanic. He tried to get me to join the Guard. He was always trying to get all of us to join the Guard. Ultimately, he convinced me that it was in my best interest to go back to school and pursue a career that was more suitable to my abilities.

He did teach me some VW tricks that stuck. Like wedging a stick between the throttle and the carburetor, which opened it up about halfway so you could get home after the accelerator cable broke. He also taught me how to get into a Bug whenever you locked your keys inside. After I stopped by for the fourth or fifth time to borrow his perpetually full five gallon military gas can because I ran out of gas, he advised me, "they run a whole lot better if you put gas in 'em to begin with."

Another trick I saw T.L. use involved jumper cables and a lot of ingenuity. The power was knocked out in their house during an ice storm. Never mind the heat, stove, washer or dryer, the TV was out. This was a disaster. Undaunted, T.L. climbed the pole out in front of the house. Using jumper cables, he managed to jump the power from the main line to the line going to the house. Problem solved. The jumper cables stayed up there for months until Georgia Power discovered them while doing routine maintenance.

T.L. put up with a lot from us as kids, more than I could have ever endured. He would pull in from work and there would be four or five jacked up hot rods parked and leaking oil on his driveway. He'd walk into his house and Foghat would be blasting from the stereo. There would be four or five teenage boys hanging around his swimming pool or running around his house in swim trunks. I would have gone postal but T.L. never did. As a matter of fact, beneath his somewhat gruff facade, you always knew he was kind, compassionate and would do anything he could to help. He helped me patch up my Bug countless times when I limped into the driveway in it. While restoring my VW convertible I sought him out constantly for advice and he gently walked me through many of the processes. When it came time to paint it, he got me the paint at his cost and let me paint it in the shop using his spray gun. He showed me the basics and I painted it myself. The end result was something less than even Earl Scheib would have claimed, but I didn't care. With T.L.'s help I had painted the car myself. I was thrilled.

Lois is without a doubt one of the funniest women I have ever known, always smiling with an infectious laugh. I have always considered her one of my best friends. One year I had to go to summer school and take a math class. It didn't help any, but that's beside the point. T.L. had bought a '67 VW bus to fix up and sell. At least twice a week I would stop by in the morning and ask Lois if I could drive the bus to school. She always let me and that's probably one of the reasons why I still covet a '67 VW Microbus today.

In the summer of 1972, T.L. and Lois took a family vacation to Panama City and invited two other friends and me to go along with them. They rented one of the old cinderblock houses on the beachfront. It was next to the Holiday Inn and a few blocks down from The Miracle Strip. It wasn't until I was grown that I realized the magnitude of that undertaking. I can only imagine taking four hormonal teenagers and three kids to the beach for a week. All week, T.L. sat on the back porch, drank beer, smoked Kools and went to the dog track at night. All these years later, I understand why.

One Saturday morning I was sitting around the pool with Lois and the younger kids. We had the radio on and they played Ray Stevens' song, The Streak. The kids disappeared inside and we heard giggling and laughing coming from the basement room. All of a sudden Sara, the youngest daughter, came running out of the room naked as a jaybird. Her two sisters, fully clothed, were right behind her screaming and laughing. She made a couple of laps around the pool. Lois and I were cheering and howling with laughter. T.L. came running down to the pool from the garage and he wasn't laughing. He yelled, "Get in that house and get your clothes back on!" Then he looked at Lois and yelled, "What's wrong with you, anyway?" We bit our lips and tried to look serious. T.L. stormed away. As soon as he left we fell out laughing again.

A group of us used to play trivia on Thursday nights at a local watering hole. One night we ran into Sara there. She slapped me on the back and said, "Hey, I just turned forty a couple of weeks ago!" I looked at her and said, "Oh, hell no. You can't turn forty. You're not allowed to turn forty." After she left and went back to her table, I looked at Beera and said, "Now does that make you feel old or what?"

Lois introduced me to mountain oysters. I was over at the house helping T.L. with the VWs. At lunchtime I walked in the kitchen and Lois was sitting talking to her friend who worked for a local vet. There were two pork chops sitting on a plate on the counter. I asked Lois, "Can I have one of these pork chops?" She looked at her friend and they both grinned. "Sure," she said, "go ahead." I ate the pork chop and said, "That was pretty good, can I have the other one?" They both fell out laughing. I stood looking at them and asked, "What's so funny? I just asked for another pork chop." When she caught her breath and could talk again, Lois said, "It's not really a pork chop. It's a mountain oyster." "What's a mountain oyster?" I asked. She told me and I must have turned forty shades of green because they started laughing even harder. I ran out of the house holding my mouth and leaving them reveling in their jocularity. I told T.L. what had happened and he started laughing too. If you don't know what a mountain oyster is, let's just say it's a certain part of a male pig's anatomy. The funny thing is, if Lois wouldn't have told me what it was, I would have eaten the second one, thought it was a pork chop, gone back outside and crawled under a VW, none the wiser.

T.L. and Lois were married for sixty six years. The last time I saw T.L. we visited him and Lois at their house in Jackson. It was a beautiful afternoon and we spent several hours laughing and reminiscing about the old times. As we were leaving, I told T.L. that I loved him. In all of the years that I had known him, it was the first and only time I had ever done so. I'm thankful now that I had that opportunity.

I don't see Lois as often as I should and that's my fault.

But I love her, T.L. and the family deeply and that will never change. They touched not only my life but also the lives of so many of the kids, teenagers, young adults and adults who lived in Gresham Park, Cedar Grove and beyond. I thank God that, in His Infinite Wisdom, he crossed my path with theirs. It is a gift for which I am forever grateful. The memories are there. They always will be.

Going Home

Several years ago Allene and I visited my stepfather in Rex. When we left, I looked at her and said, "Let's ride through the old neighborhoods in East Atlanta and Gresham Park." We headed up Moreland Avenue toward our respective hometowns.

First we rode through East Atlanta. We turned off of Moreland onto Glenwood and drove past what used to be Charlie's Place. My father and I ate there quite a bit when I was a kid. Charlie would soak the meat in his chili, pull it out, flatten it to a patty and cook it to order. I would have a hamburger and a Nehi chocolate drink. Daddy would have a dressed dog, which was a hot dog split, placed on an open bun and topped with chili. The building is now painted gray and Charlie's Place sits empty.

We turned onto Florida Avenue and stopped in front of my grandparents' house. The street was much narrower than I remembered and I commented to Allene that I didn't know how they navigated the narrow streets in the big cars of the mid-twentieth century. My grandparents' house looked fairly good, although a little rough around the edges. My grandfather's garage and the "Little House," which was the efficiency apartment attached to the garage, were both gone. I looked at the front porch where I used to sit and shell peas with my Mema and play with my cousins. It looked much smaller than I remembered.

We continued up the street and passed the last house on the right of Florida Avenue. The house had an arched stone entrance and fireplace and looked very much as it always had, neat, clean and tidy. Our house was two stories and was located at the corner of Sanders Avenue and Florida Avenue. My aunt, uncle and cousins lived behind our two-story house. Our old house looked rough. It had been restored at one point in the Nineties but now looked to be derelict again. The screened in porch on the side of the house was open, the big back yard overgrown with vegetation. In contrast, the house behind ours where my cousins lived had been renovated and it, too, was nice and clean.

We drove back through East Atlanta, turned onto Cloverdale Drive and into the old Sky Haven neighborhood. We drove down Elmhurst Circle and stopped in front of the big brick house that my uncle built, which was where my other cousins lived. The house was in beautiful shape and still looked exactly the same as it had in our childhood. My uncle knew how to build things to last. We rode past Sky Haven School. It was empty and would soon fall victim to the wrecking ball, like so many of the older DeKalb County schools. We turned off of Ripplewater Drive and headed up Eastland Road toward the house where Allene grew up. Her old house had been completely renovated and looked great. The roof on the garage in the back, where her dad worked on VWs, had been replaced with glass panels and was apparently being used as a greenhouse.

We then rode down Brannen Road and into Gresham Park. The hills that seemed so steep as a kid now appeared rolling and gentle. The houses appeared to be a lot smaller as well, just like my grandmother's street and the front porch in East Atlanta. I suppose everything looks bigger when you're a kid.

We turned up Boulder Road and stopped at the top of the hill in front of Gresham Park Elementary School. I had heard the stories but refused to believe them. The stories were true. The school had been torn down. I got out of the car and peered through the makeshift chain link fence. My heart sank and a wave of sadness came over me along with a flood of memories. The destruction was not complete at that particular time. The only thing that was left standing was the inside wall of the lunchroom. It was the wall we were in front of when our seventh grade graduation picture was taken. Everything else was a pile of rubble. "Do you want to get a brick?" Allene asked me. There were *No Trespassing* signs on the fence. I thought about it for a second and then said, "No, I don't want to risk getting arrested." "I'm going back to the car," she said. "Take as much time as you need."

I have heard people say that they have no regrets in life

and that past mistakes helped make them what they are today. I can understand that, but I have regrets and lots of them. Given the opportunity, there are many things that I would go back and do differently. Near the top of that list is not climbing that stupid fence, walking across that pile of debris and collecting a brick from the building that, for nine months out of each year, was the center of the universe.

I stared for a long time at the place where the school once stood. I could still see it. I could see the piles of newspapers stacked up along the front wall of the building for the PTA paper drive. I could see the backstops, the playgrounds and the basketball court. I could see the school carnival going on and me giving rides in my Briggs and Stratton powered miniature T-Model. I remembered how thrilled I was when The Girl climbed in and I gave her a ride to the end of the schoolyard and back. I could see the big thick burgundy velvet curtain in front of the stage and smell the food in the lunchroom. Gresham Park Elementary was still there. But it wasn't. It was torn down and gone. I walked back to the car, climbed in and started it up. The tears suddenly welled up in my eyes and started to flow. "It's like a huge portion of my childhood and my life and the lives of lots of others has been wiped away," I said to Allene. "Why? What for? Progress? Blanking progress. Maybe sometimes the best progress is leaving things the way they are."

I collected myself and we drove down Flintwood Drive past The Girl's house and turned onto Rollingwood Lane. The hill going down to the bottom was still a big hill. It was not rolling nor was it subtle. We passed Bubba-Bubba's house on the left and the flood plain that was our football field. It wasn't much of a flood plain anymore. It was covered with weeds and briars and there was an abandoned above-ground swimming pool at the far end. The woods were ravaged with kudzu and you could see all the way through to the street behind us. We rode up the hill past Anna's house on the right and stopped in front of my house. It looked okay. Not great, but not dilapidated. I peered through the kudzu encroaching on the left side of the house and could make out the shapes of the iron clothesline poles that my father had welded together in the early Sixties. I could not believe that they were still standing. There was a car parked in the driveway. "Do you want to knock on the door and ask to see inside?" Allene asked. "No," I answered. "I'm afraid to. Not afraid to knock on the door, but of what I might see inside. I'd rather remember it the way that it was." That's a decision I don't regret.

I turned and looked at Billy's house across the street. It looked to be in about the same shape as ours. Rough, but livable. We continued up the hill past Brain's house, which appeared to be abandoned. We crossed over Boulderview Drive and took a right onto Mary

Lou Lane. Pointing out houses of different friends, we made our way down to Bouldercrest Road. We took a right and pulled into the home of the McNair Mustangs, formerly known as Walker High School.

We parked in the front lot. The school was unrecognizable. Ornate facades were all along the buildings, the front entrance to the school and what was once the gym. Our old gym had become a performing arts center and a big new gym had been built on what was once the baseball field. We walked up to the new gym and out in front were huge statues of horses rearing up. "It looks like something out of Las Vegas," said Allene, peering up at one of the statues. "Look, the tennis courts are still in the same place," I said, pointing at the courts on the hill behind the old gym. A new wing of classrooms had been built where there was once woods and the infamous old Smoking Tree. The building reached all the way to Mary Lou Lane.

We pulled out of the lot, drove to the other side of the school and pulled into what was once the student parking lot, a.k.a. Smoke City. As we turned in, Allene pointed at a street sign at the top of the lot and exclaimed, "Look! The parking lot's called Walker Way!" So, that was the only reference to the old school. I laughed and thought it apropos that Smoke City and the lot where so many awesome cars were once parked was now named Walker Way.

The new building extended all the way to the edge of the parking lot. There were a few parking places marked out but not many. We drove to the bottom of Walker Way and parked. A baseball field and softball field were now where the old gravel lot and part of the football practice field once sat. As we stood and looked at the baseball field I said to Allene, "You know, it's better to see it like this than condemned and torn down." "Yes, I know," she said, "but I can still see our school in there." "I know, Honey," I said, "so can I."

We pulled out of the lot and headed for home. As I was driving, it occurred to me that we were not headed for home at all. We were leaving our home. The neighborhoods that we had ridden through were not just houses in which we had lived. Those were our homes and our hometowns. And in them we laughed. We cried. We lived. We died. We won. We lost. We experienced joy. We experienced heartbreak. We worked. We played. We had disagreements. We had understandings. We were praised. We were punished. We learned firsthand to live life. We grew up. And the memories are there. They always will be.

21313513R00077

Made in the USA
Lexington, KY
10 December 2018